CALIFORNIA
Finfish and Shellfish
IDENTIFICATION
BOOK

A Companion Guide to the California Fishing Passport

W9-CXW-221

State of California
The Resources Agency
Department of Fish and Wildlife

Edmund G. Brown, Jr.
Governor

John Laird
Secretary for Resources

Charlton H. Bonham
Department of Fish and Wildlife Director

Lead Editors: Mary Patyten, Edgar W. Roberts III,
Mike Giusti, Walt Beer, Roger Bloom, Mike Harris,
Carrie Wilson

Layout and design by Mary Patyten

California Department of Fish and Wildlife
Copyright © 2015 California Department of Fish and Wildlife.
All rights reserved.
Third printing, July 2015.
Printed in the United States of America
ISBN 0-9722291-1-6

California is home

to a great diversity of freshwater and saltwater finfish and shellfish. With this in mind, the California Department of Fish and Wildlife (CDFW) developed the California Fishing Passport program to highlight and promote the tremendous fishing resources that are available and unique to California.

The *California Finfish and Shellfish Identification Book* serves not only as a companion guide to the California Fishing Passport, it also stands on its own merits. With comprehensive information for people to use as they fish their way throughout the state in pursuit of all of the species included in the program, and detailed illustrations by top artists Amadeo Bachar, Joseph Tomelleri (see page 176), and Jeremy Taylor, readers should find this to be a great resource guide for California's many different fisheries for years to come. All of the species featured in the program and in this book are those that we have found to be most important to the anglers, divers and outdoor sports enthusiasts of California.

Much of the content and material for this book comes from CDFW publications and staff experts. Each entry provides specific information about a fish or invertebrate as it occurs in California. We hope that the *California Finfish and Shellfish Identification Book* will provide an exciting peek into the many opportunities that await anglers of all ages here in California.

Acknowledgements

The *California Finfish and Shellfish Identification Book* has been made possible through the collaborative efforts of numerous staff members within CDFW. It is a compilation of current information gleaned from numerous resources and from the professionals involved in the California Fishing Passport program. Many CDFW biologists and personnel contributed to writing and reviewing the text and illustrations. Special thanks go to Walter Beer, Roger Bloom, Michael Giusti, Michael Harris, Dennis Lee, Joseph Millosovich, David Moore, Mary Patyten, Ed Roberts III, and Carrie Wilson. Important contributions were also made by Kristine Barsky, Michael Connell, Jack Crayon, Aaron Del Monte, Bernadette Fees, Steven Goldman, Michelle Horeczko, Peter Kalvass, Konstantin Karpov, Jerry Kashiwada, Sharon Keeney, Dave Lentz, Neil Manji, Sonke Mastrup, Darlene McGriff, Stephanie Mehalick, Ken Oda, Curtis Milliron, Katie Perry, Mike Prall, Paul Reilly, Alexia Retallack, Ethan Rotman, Travis Tanaka, John Ugoretz, Stephen Wertz, and Brian Young.

Finally, we would like to express our profound thanks to the authors of previous CDFW guidebooks and publications, including *Warmwater Game Fishes of California*, *Anadromous Fishes of California*, *Trout of California*, *Marine Sportfish Identification*, *Inshore Fishes of California*, *Offshore Fishes of California*, and *California's Living Marine Resources: A Status Report*. The bulk of this book's content was derived and updated from these earlier publications. It is our intent that the *California Finfish and Shellfish Identification Book* continue CDFW's tradition of public outreach and education.

List of Species

Inland Warmwater Fishes

Inland Coldwater Fishes

Inland Shellfish

Anadromous Fishes

Ocean Fishes

Ocean Shellfish

California Fishing Passport Resources

California Fishing Passport Home Page

www.fishingpassport.org

The California Fishing Passport program's home page is the central hub for "all things Passport." Here you'll find lots of useful information about the program, including:

- How the program works
- Awards for different levels of achievement
- Dates of future California Fishing Passport Challenge events & Passport Challenge news
- Where to get a passport and a finfish & shellfish identification book
- Information about California Fishing Passport Sponsors
- Where to get your passport stamped
- Links to CDFW's Online Fishing Guide (below)

For more information about the California Fishing Passport program, check with your local CDFW office or e-mail program staff at passport@wildlife.ca.gov.

Department of Fish and Wildlife Online Fishing Guide

www.fishingpassport.org/FishingGuide

Plan your fishing trip with help from CDFW's **Online Fishing Guide**, which contains hundreds of great recreational fishing locations throughout the state, information about the fish species available, and the services found at various locations.

Proper Method for Catch and Release

The Department of Fish and Wildlife encourages anglers to exercise care when they fish freshwater "catch and release" waters or land non-target species. When anglers catch and release fish that are too large, too small, or are restricted species, proper handling of the fish helps to protect and preserve California's fish populations.

For all species, these general guidelines apply for both tackle and technique:
• Use unscented artificial lures (no bait) to minimize deep hooking. Barbless hooks or hooks with flattened barbs make unhooking easier and less stressful on the fish.
• Avoid stainless steel hooks.
• Avoid and replace treble hooks on lures, especially with saltwater species.
• Land fish as carefully and quickly as possible; avoid playing the fish to exhaustion.
• Use an appropriate-sized landing net to assist in catching, handling, and releasing the fish. Knotless small-mesh nets are easiest on fish.
• Try to avoid removing the fish from the water.

Once a fish is landed, these steps will help reduce stress on the fish:
• Use wet hands or wet cotton gloves when handling the fish.
• Do not squeeze the fish or touch its eyes or gills.
• Quickly remove only those hooks that are seen and removed easily. Clip the line near the mouth on deeply hooked fish. Underwater unhooking and release is best.
• Avoid having the fish hit the deck of the boat or flop around on the shore.
• Minimize the time the fish is out of the water.

For reviving and releasing the fish:
• Hold the fish horizontally and upright facing into the current.
• Gently move the fish forward and backwards until it swims away on its own.
• For fish that have buoyancy issues, have a release device (such as a weighted plastic crate) on hand and ready.

Fish Diagram

Diagram of a hypothetical fish, showing features mentioned in the text
(Not all of these features will be found on any one kind of fish)

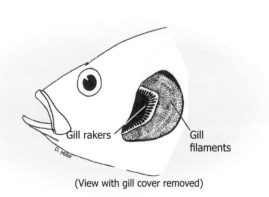

adapted from diagram by P. Johnson

(View with gill cover removed)

*W*armwater inland fishing in California covers a broad range of fish and fishing techniques. At one extreme is the simplicity of a youngster fishing for bluegill in a farm pond with a willow pole and a worm on a hook. At the other end of the scale may be the finesse and sophistication of a tournament bass angler in search of a 'kicker' fish, tearing across the lake in a fiberglass boat full of a variety of rods and reels, fish finders, and the latest custom-colored handmade artificial lures.

Many young anglers have been introduced to the sport at a lake or pond stocked with a good population of "panfish." These smaller members of the sunfish family are plentiful in many waters and can provide fast action even for inexperienced anglers. In addition to being fun to catch, they are excellent eating. Many youngsters have become lifelong anglers as a result of not only catching their first fish, but putting dinner on the table as well.

The common link among warmwater fishing experiences is that the angler targets fish that prefer water temperatures generally too warm for trout. This is not to say that trout and warmwater fish cannot occur in the same body of water. Many of California's lakes and reservoirs support excellent "two-story" fisheries where warmwater species such as bass and sunfish can be caught in warmer surface waters, and trout in deeper, cooler areas.

California Fishing Passport

California's traditional warmwater gamefish include one native species, the Sacramento perch, and 18 introduced, non-native species. The non-native fish include largemouth, smallmouth, spotted, and redeye bass; bluegill, warmouth, green, pumpkinseed, and redear sunfish; white and black crappie; channel, white, blue, and flathead catfish; and yellow, brown, and black bullhead. In addition to traditional gamefish, California inland anglers may also try their hand fishing for landlocked striped bass, white bass, yellow perch, native tule perch, carp, and tilapia.

Because most members of this group are aggressive and very prolific, they can have negative effects on native fish populations. Remember that transplanting live fish may not only be bad for native fish, it is illegal without a CDFW permit.

Warmwater fish can be found throughout California in urban and rural streams, rivers, ponds, lakes, and reservoirs, and can provide excellent sport and good table fare. Warmwater fish have not only introduced lots of people to the sport of fishing, they can provide a lifetime of angling challenges.

Largemouth Bass

to ~30 in.

The largemouth bass
is one of California's most popular inland warmwater species. The timing of its arrival in California is uncertain, since it may have been included with plantings of smallmouth bass in Napa and Alameda creeks in 1874. Largemouth bass have been present in California since at least 1895.

In 1959, a sub-species of largemouth bass from Florida was introduced into San Diego County lakes, where the fish has attained exceptional size. Florida largemouth were introduced into Clear Lake, Lake County in 1969 and numerous California waters since then where they have hybridized with existing populations of the northern sub-species.

Distinguishing Characteristics
Upper jaw extends past a vertical line drawn through the rear margin of eye; dark, blotchy longitudinal bands on sides, less prominent in old individuals; dorsal fin deeply notched when compared to smallmouth bass.

Life History & Other Notes
Largemouth bass prefer warm water, usually in excess of 65° F. They become lethargic and lose their appetite when the water is colder than 50° F, and remain in deep water in a torpid state for much of the winter. As the water warms they move into the shallows, and when the temperature rises to 60° to 65° F in the spring they begin spawning.

Largemouth Bass

SCIENTIFIC NAME
Micropterus salmoides

OTHER COMMON NAMES
bigmouth bass, bucketmouth

RANGE & HABITAT
Statewide in nearly all suitable lakes, sloughs, slow-moving rivers, ponds

LENGTH & WEIGHT
To ~30 in. and 21+ lb.

LIFESPAN
To 16 years

DIET & SUGGESTED BAIT/LURES
Feeds on threadfin shad, bluegills, crayfish. Try lures that resemble shad or bluegill, or plastic worms

---

Redeye Bass

— to 15 in. —

In 1962 and 1964, redeye bass from Tennessee and Georgia were introduced into five small streams in central and Southern California. Reproducing populations developed in the South Fork of the Stanislaus River, Tuolumne County, and in the Santa Margarita River in San Diego County. Reproducing populations are also present in Lake Oroville where they were planted in 1968, and in New Melones Reservoir which impounded fish from the Stanislaus River. Their typical habitat includes small streams that are too warm for trout, and too small or too cold for other basses.

Distinguishing Characteristics

Fins and eyes of adults are brick red. May exhibit blue or greenish cast to the body, and white margins on the tail and anal fins. Often mistaken for smallmouth bass, but is more closely related to spotted bass. Young redeye bass may be distinguished from other black basses by red fins and the absence of a black band across the lobes of the tail fin.

Life History & Other Notes

Redeye bass were brought into California to fill a niche unoccupied by any other game species. They are opportunistic feeders much like trout, but are extremely slow growing compared to other basses. They rarely exceed 15 inches in length. Spawning behavior is similar to that of the smallmouth bass, except that spawning occurs when water temperatures reach 62° to 70° F.

Redeye Bass

SCIENTIFIC NAME
Micropterus coosae

OTHER COMMON NAMES
coosa bass, shoal bass

RANGE & HABITAT
Primarily in northern and central California lakes and small streams

LENGTH & WEIGHT
To 15 in. and ~5 lb.

LIFESPAN
To 10 years

DIET & SUGGESTED BAIT/LURES
Feeds on aquatic insects, fish, crayfish, salamanders. Try small crankbaits, jigs and plastic worms

15

Smallmouth Bass

to 18 in.

The smallmouth bass was first brought to California in 1874 from Lake Champlain, Vermont and the St. Joseph River, Michigan, and planted in the Napa River and Alameda Creek. It subsequently spread and was introduced into a number of waters throughout central and northern California. It is now found, among other places, in Trinity Lake, Putah Creek, the Russian River, the Colorado River, Pyramid Lake, Diamond Valley Lake, the lower portions of Sacramento and San Joaquin river tributaries, and many Central Valley impoundments such as Shasta Lake, Shasta County; Oroville Lake, Butte County, and Folsom Lake, Placer and El Dorado counties. Smallmouth bass prefer lower temperatures (about 70° F) and adapt to swifter currents than largemouth bass. They do best in clear, boulder-strewn streams with large pools, and in clear lakes with scant vegetation and rocky shoal areas for spawning.

Distinguishing Characteristics
Dark vertical barring usually present on sides. Upper jaw does not extend to rear margin of eye and dorsal fin is not deeply notched.

Life History & Other Notes
Smallmouth bass are the earliest spawning bass, beginning in the spring when water temperatures reach 55° to 60° F.

Smallmouth are an aggressive bass that will go after all types of bass lures, particularly jigs. They are often considered better fighters than largemouth bass. Most anglers are very satisfied with catching a 2- to 3-lb. smallmouth bass.

Smallmouth Bass

SCIENTIFIC NAME
Micropterus dolomieu

OTHER COMMON NAMES
bronzeback, smallies, brown bass

RANGE & HABITAT
Statewide in clear streams, lakes with rocky areas

LENGTH & WEIGHT
To 25 in. and ~9 lb.

LIFESPAN
To 15 years

DIET & SUGGESTED LURES
Feeds on fish, amphibians, small mammals, crayfish. Try crayfish colored crankbaits, jigs, spinnerbaits, or plastic worms

Spotted Bass

to ~26 in.

Northern spotted bass were flown to California in 1933 from Ohio, reared at the Department's Central Valley Hatchery, and planted in several lakes and ponds. They have become established in a limited portion of the Cosumnes River in Sacramento and El Dorado counties; Merle Collins Lake, Yuba County; and Oroville Lake and the Feather River below it, Butte County. In 1974, 95 Alabama spotted bass from Lewis Smith Reservoir, Alabama were planted in Lake Perris, Riverside County. Progeny from this plant have subsequently become established in numerous California reservoirs, where they appear to be quite successful in adapting to large fluctuations in water level. Spotted bass prefer to inhabit the open water portion of lakes more than largemouth or smallmouth bass.

Distinguishing Characteristics
Upper jaw extends to rear margin of eye. Blotchy lateral band with spots above it and linear streaks below. Dorsal fin not deeply notched.

Life History & Other Notes
Spotted bass feed on sunfish, crappie and threadfin shad, depending on seasonal availability.

Spotted bass begin spawning in the spring when water temperatures reach 57° to 74° F, and are not as prolific as other black basses. They are normally slower-growing than largemouth bass. The northern form rarely exceeds 3 lb., while the Alabama form has a higher growth potential: 4- to 5-lb. fish are not uncommon, although 2-lb. fish are the rule in California.

Spotted Bass
SCIENTIFIC NAME
Micropterus punctulatus

OTHER COMMON NAMES
spot, spottie, Alabama spotted bass

RANGE & HABITAT
Primarily in northern and central California lakes and rivers

LENGTH & WEIGHT
To ~26 in. and 10 lb.

LIFESPAN
To 5 years

DIET & SUGGESTED BAIT/LURES
Feeds on fish including sunfish, crappie, and threadfin shad. Try topwater lures, crankbaits, or Carolina rigging plastic worms.

17

White Bass

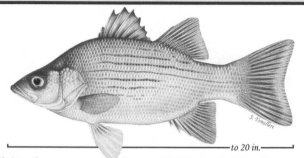

— to 20 in. —

White bass are native

to central North American waterways and drainages. They were first introduced into Lake Nacimiento, San Luis Obispo County in 1965 from Nebraska. Additional lots from Oklahoma, Utah, and Nevada were stocked in the reservoir in 1966, 1967, and 1968. At first, no reproduction was evident, but by the summer of 1971, white bass dominated the fishery. In the late 1960s, they were introduced into the lower Colorado River, but apparently did not reproduce as they are not caught there now. A few of the originally planted fish were taken, however, including the current state record white bass.

White bass prefer deep water habitat over sand, gravel and rocky areas. On sunny days, the fish stay offshore in deep water to feed on threadfin shad until just before dark when they move closer to shore.

Distinguishing Characteristics

Body silvery, sides with about seven longitudinal stripes. Dorsal fins separate. Body is deeper than striped bass. Mouth is crappie-like.

Life History & Other Notes

White bass were illegally intro duced into Kaweah Lake, Tular County, where a self-sustainin population became established This population was eliminated b chemical treatment in 1987 becaus of potential damage to the spor fishery in Delta waters, shoul white bass become establishe there. This is one of the few specie of fish which by law must be kille immediately when taken.

White Bass

SCIENTIFIC NAME
Morone chrysops

OTHER COMMON NAMES
silver bass, sand bass, white perch

RANGE & HABITAT
Lake Nacimiento

LENGTH & WEIGHT
To 20 in. and ~5 lb.

LIFESPAN
To ~9 years

DIET & SUGGESTED BAIT/LURES
Feeds on small fish including threadfin shad. Try topwater lures, spinners, small crankbaits, spoons, flies, and jigs, or use shad for bait

Black Bullhead

to ~10 in.

The black bullhead

has been reported to inhabit several widely scattered waters throughout the State, though its distribution may be even greater. It is possible that the black bullhead may have been overlooked because of its close resemblance to the brown bullhead. Records of its introduction are not clear but it was probably introduced in 1874 with other Mississippi Valley catfishes into the Sacramento and San Joaquin rivers. It was first reported in the Colorado River in 1942. Some fishable populations are present in large, low elevation lakes and reservoirs. Black bullheads prefer warmwater ponds, sloughs, and sluggish streams. They are often found in shallow and silty water and are highly tolerant of warm water and pollutants.

Distinguishing Characteristics
Coloration similar to that of brown bullhead, but usually not mottled. Fin membranes generally black. Pectoral spine weakly barbed on rear edge; spine offers little resistance when grasped by thumb and forefinger. Tail square; not deeply forked. Belly frequently brassy or golden.

Life History & Other Notes
During reproduction, adult brown bullheads guard the eggs and then the young until the fry are about 1 in. long. Though populations in small lakes and reservoirs often become stunted, the black bullhead can grow to over 10 in. long.

Black Bullhead
SCIENTIFIC NAME
Ameiurus melas
OTHER COMMON NAMES
mudcat, black catfish, bullhead

RANGE & HABITAT
*Statewide in warmwater ponds,
sloughs, sluggish streams,
shallow areas*

LENGTH & WEIGHT
To ~10 in. and ~1 lb.
LIFESPAN
To 10 years

DIET & SUGGESTED BAIT
*Feeds on insects, worms, mollusks,
fish eggs, fish, algae. Try using red
worms or night crawlers for bait*

19

Brown Bullhead

to ~10 in.

The brown bullhead

is the most widely distributed member of the catfish family, and occurs in most suitable warmwater areas statewide. It was first planted in 1874 from Lake Champlain, Vermont, in ponds and sloughs near Sacramento. Brown bullhead prefer deep, weedy waters with sand, gravel, or mud substrates in warmwater ponds, lakes, or sluggish streams.

Distinguishing Characteristics

Back more or less dark brown, belly gray to yellowish; sides and back typically mottled. Pectoral spine strongly barbed on rear edge; spine offers resistance when grasped by thumb and forefinger; tail square-ish; not deeply forked. The membrane between the tail rays is clear, not colored as with the black bullhead.

Life History & Other Notes

Brown bullhead can live in waters with temperatures between 32° and 98° F, although optimum growth occurs at temperatures between 68° and 95° F. They can tolerate relatively low oxygen levels.

Brown bullhead feed near the bottom throughout the day. Sexual maturity is reached at age 3, and spawning occurs when water temperatures near 70° F. Nests are built in sand or mud in shallow weedy areas. The parents protect both the eggs and the young for several weeks after hatching. At hatching, the young are black and about ¼ in. long. This fish is very prolific and often overproduce with the resultant population becoming stunted.

Brown Bullhead

SCIENTIFIC NAME
Ameiurus nebulosus

OTHER COMMON NAMES
creek cat, mud cat, brown catfish

RANGE & HABITAT
Statewide, especially in warmwater ponds, lakes, sluggish streams; deep areas with aquatic vegetation

LENGTH & WEIGHT
To ~ 10 in. and ~1 pound

LIFESPAN
To 11 years

DIET & SUGGESTED BAIT
Fish, crayfish, algae, fish eggs, insects, leeches. Try red worms or night crawlers for bait

Yellow Bullhead

J. Tomelleri

to 13+ in.

As with the black bullhead, the timing of the yellow bullhead's introduction is unclear. It may have been introduced in 1874 with other Mississippi Valley catfishes into the Sacramento and San Joaquin rivers; remnants of this planting are still present in small numbers in adjacent sloughs. Yellow bullhead are now largely restricted to the Colorado River drainage, having become established there sometime before 1942 when it was first reported. It may also exist in a few Southern California reservoirs and has been reported from Lost River, Modoc County.

The yellow bullhead prefers the shallow portions of lakes, ponds, and low gradient streams. It is found in clear water where there is an abundance of aquatic vegetation.

Distinguishing Characteristics

Color is variable. Back several shades of brown to almost black; belly more or less yellow. Tail rounded, not forked. Chin barbels whitish, compared with the gray to black barbels of brown and black bullheads. Anal fin ray count 24 to 27 compared with 17 to 24 in brown and black bullheads.

Life History & Other Notes

Yellow bullheads usually mature in their third year. Spawning habits resemble those of other bullheads, except that the males guard the young until they are about 2 in. long. Yellow bullhead can grow to lengths of over 13 in.

Yellow Bullhead

SCIENTIFIC NAME
Ameiurus natalis

OTHER COMMON NAMES
*white-whiskered bullhead,
yellow belly*

RANGE & HABITAT
Colorado River and isolated lakes in Southern California, in shallows

LENGTH & WEIGHT
To 13+ in. and ~3 lb.

LIFESPAN
Estimated to 11 years

DIET & SUGGESTED BAIT
Insects, worms, mollusks, fish eggs, fish, plants. Try red worms or night crawlers for bait

Blue Catfish

J. Tomelleri

— to 55+ in. —

Blue catfish were introduced into Lake Jennings, San Diego County, from Stuttgart, Arkansas by the Department in 1969. Since then, the species has been introduced into Sutherland Reservoir, El Capitan Reservoir, San Vicente Reservoir, and the Santee Lake chain, San Diego County. Blue catfish are also present in small numbers in the Sacramento-San Joaquin Delta.

Distinguishing Characteristics

Easily confused with the channel catfish because of similar shape, coloration, and presence of spots on young. Can be distinguished by a fin ray count of 30 to 35 in the anal fin, and by a more pronounced, angular rise to the back, originating just behind the head and continuing to the base of the dorsal fin. The anal fin, which extends for about one-third the length of the body, distinguishes it from the white catfish.

Life History & Other Notes

Blue catfish, the largest of the American catfishes, may reach over 100 lb. in its native range (large rivers from Minnesota and Ohio southward into Mexico).

22

Although growth is best at water temperatures over 80° F, they can withstand temperatures from 32° to 98° F. Spawning occurs in June and early July at water temperatures of about 70° to 75° F. Nests similar to those of the channel catfish are constructed under overhanging rock ledges, along deeply undercut banks, and in other sheltered places. Feeding habits are generally similar to those of the bottom-feeding channel catfish.

Blue Catfish

SCIENTIFIC NAME
Ictalurus furcatus

OTHER COMMON NAMES
forktail cat, humpback blue

RANGE & HABITAT
Primarily large rivers and lakes in Southern California and infrequently in the Sacramento Delta

LENGTH & WEIGHT
To 55+ in. and 100+ lb.

LIFESPAN
Estimated to 25 years

DIET & SUGGESTED BAIT
Insects, worms, leeches, snails, crayfish, fish. Try cut mackerel or anchovies, or live fish for bait

Channel Catfish

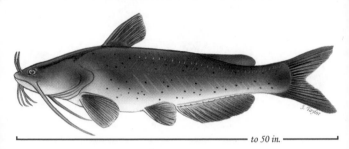

— to 50 in. —

In recent years, the channel catfish has been stocked in many large and small reservoirs. Early records indicate that in 1874 fish originating from the Mississippi Valley were introduced into the San Joaquin River near Stockton. In 1891, channel catfish were planted in Lake Cuyamaca, San Diego County, and in the Feather River, but only the Feather River plant was successful. The channel catfish is one of the most abundant species of catfish in the Colorado River. It was first documented there in 1932, although steamboat captains' logbooks report channel catfish in the river before 1909. Channel catfish appear in substantial numbers in the Sacramento River drainage, especially in the Sutter Bypass.

Distinguishing Characteristics
Bluish on back, whitish below and on sides. Easily confused with blue and white catfish, but can be distinguished by one or more of the following features: small irregular spots on sides, which may be obscure or absent in large fish; tail deeply forked with pointed lobes; 24 to 29 rays in anal fin. Head relatively narrow compared to the broad head of the white catfish.

Life History & Other Notes
Channel catfish are very active, and can grow quite large (over 50 lb.). Their size and excellent eating qualities make them prized sport fish. Channel catfish spend their days in deep holes, under logs or other shelter, and feed in shallow water at night. They attain a larger size in water temperatures of 70° F or warmer.

Channel Catfish
SCIENTIFIC NAME
Ictalurus punctatus
OTHER COMMON NAMES
spotted cat, channel cat, river cat
RANGE & HABITAT
Statewide in warmwater reservoirs and larger river systems with wood or stone structure
LENGTH & WEIGHT
To 50 in. and 52+ lb.
LIFESPAN
To 20 years
DIET & SUGGESTED BAIT
Feeds mostly on fish, crayfish, aquatic insects. Try frozen anchovies, chicken livers or other "stink baits"

23

Flathead Catfish

— *to 4+ ft.* —

Flathead catfish were

introduced into the Colorado River near Yuma in 1962 by the Arizona Game and Fish Department. The species spread upstream in the Colorado River to the Blythe area and have moved throughout the Imperial Valley canal system. Young-of-the-year were captured in the Highline Canal and several water supply ditches in California's Imperial Valley during early 1968. In 1980, a flathead catfish was captured in the Bill Williams Arm of Lake Havasu, San Bernadino County, 162 miles upstream of the original introduction site. Recently flathead catfish have been seen at Lake Skinner and Lake Perris in Riverside County. Flathead catfish are found mainly in large, muddy rivers and reservoirs, and often prefer deep holes.

Distinguishing Characteristics

Coloration generally brown, with dark brown to olive and yellow mottlings on back and upper sides. Abdomen much lighter. Tail squared, only slightly forked. Head broad and flat compared to other catfishes. Lower jaw longer than upper. Anal fin with 14 to 17 rays.

Life History & Other Notes

Flathead catfish are mostly nocturnal feeders. Spawning occurs in early summer. Nests are built in large depressions either in river banks or against logs and submerged obstructions. In the Colorado River, several fish in the 50-lb. class were recorded in 1980. Fish weighing 20 lb. are not uncommon. In their native Midwest, flathead catfish can sometimes weigh up to 100 lb.

Flathead Catfish

SCIENTIFIC NAME
Pylodictis olivaris
OTHER COMMON NAMES
shovelhead cat, yellow cat

RANGE & HABITAT
Primarily the Colorado River and canals/drains of Imperial and Coachella valleys; prefers large muddy rivers and reservoirs.
LENGTH & WEIGHT
To 4+ ft. and 100 lb.
LIFESPAN
To 25 years

DIET & SUGGESTED BAIT
Eats insect larvae, crayfish, mollusks, worms, fish. Try live fish for bait

White Catfish

— to 24 in. —

The white catfish is abundant in California, where it is found in most suitable warm waters. About 95 percent of the catfish caught in the Sacramento-San Joaquin Delta are white catfish. They were introduced into the San Joaquin River near Stockton in 1874, from the Raritan River, New Jersey. White catfish inhabit a variety of fresh or slightly brackish waters, usually preferring water 70° F or warmer. They do well in both fresh and brackish water, in large reservoirs, small ponds, and slow-moving rivers.

Distinguishing Characteristics

Bluish to grayish above and silvery below. Tail deeply forked, 19 to 23 rays in the anal fin.

Life History & Other Notes

As with most catfish, white catfish are mainly carnivorous; fish, fish eggs, insects, crustaceans, mollusks, and frogs contribute to their diet.

White catfish in California generally attain sexual maturity at 7 to 8 inches in length, during their third or fourth year of life. They spawn in the summer when water temperatures reach 70° F, and lay their eggs in nests that may be covered with gravel. One or both parents guard the eggs; the male cares for the young. They are a very popular sport fish on the Sacramento-San Joaquin Delta.

White Catfish

SCIENTIFIC NAME
Ameiurus catus

OTHER COMMON NAMES
Fork-tailed cat, silver cat

RANGE & HABITAT
Statewide in reservoirs, large, slow moving rivers, ponds, and brackish waters

LENGTH & WEIGHT
To 24 in. and 22 lb.

LIFESPAN
To ~11 years

DIET & SUGGESTED BAIT
Feeds on fish, insects, mollusks, crustaceans, frogs, fish eggs. Try cut fish and "stink baits"

25

Common Carp

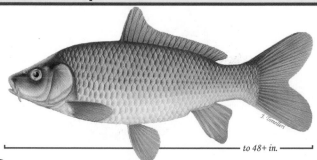

◄─────────────────── to 48+ in. ───►

Common carp were first introduced to California in 1872, when five fish imported from Holstein, Germany were planted in Sonoma County ponds. Carp were soon raised in large numbers for food. They now thrive in all of the lowland waters of the Central Valley, nearly all Southern California reservoirs, the Colorado River, and many small coastal drainages, as well as on the east slope of the Sierra Nevada.

Distinguishing Characteristics

Body color ranges from brassy green to golden or brassy yellow to silver. Humped, heavy, broad in appearance. Long dorsal fin, the first ray of which is a heavy, toothed spine. A similar spine occurs in the anal fin. The upper jaw has two barbels on each side.

Life History & Other Notes

Carp eat animal matter, plant material, and mud. They are "rooters" and often keep the bottom stirred up so that the water remains muddy. They enter the shallows in large numbers to spawn during the spring. At this time they can be seen splashing and rolling with their backs out of the water. Carp

are prolific breeders, with females of 15 to 20 lb. producing 2 million eggs each season.

Carp are often considered pests because they destroy aquatic plants used by waterfowl and because they roil the water, causing silt-sensitive game fish to seek clearer waters. Even so, a growing number of fishermen regularly seek out carp for food and sport. A favorite bait consists of corn flakes mashed with strawberry jam, presented on a small treble hook.

Common Carp

SCIENTIFIC NAME
Cyprinus carpio

OTHER COMMON NAMES
German carp, European carp

RANGE & HABITAT
Statewide in lakes, reservoirs, rivers, ponds, and brackish waters

LENGTH & WEIGHT
To 48+ in. and 80 lb.

LIFESPAN
To 47 years

DIET & SUGGESTED BAIT/LURES
Feeds on aquatic plants and invertebrates. Try dough balls on small treble hooks, or flies. For best results use light line and no weight

---

Black Crappie

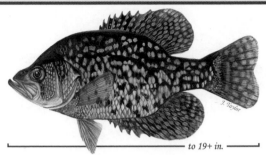

to 19+ in.

Although planting records for crappie are vague, it is likely that the first successful black crappie plant was in 1908, when fish from Meredosia, Illinois were planted in Clear Lake, Lake County and sloughs and oxbows of the Feather, Sacramento, San Joaquin, Kings and Kern rivers. They were also distributed into waters in Ventura, Los Angeles, Riverside, and Orange counties. They are now the most widespread of the two crappie species, occurring in most suitable waters throughout California.

Distinguishing Characteristics
Silvery with irregular dark green or black mottling. Length of dorsal fin base about equal to distance from front of dorsal fin to eye. Seven or eight dorsal fin spines.

Life History & Other Notes
Adult black crappie are fish-eaters. They need abundant forage fish coupled with heavy fishing to provide and maintain a desirable fishery. Without heavy fishing, they tend to overpopulate an area and become stunted. Under favorable conditions, black crappie reach 4 lb., but crappie of half a pound or so are more common. Crappie tend to gather in schools in the shelter of submerged stumps and brush heaps during the nesting season, which begins in May or June. These brush areas can provide excellent fishing during this time of year. The black crappie is one of the few members of the sunfish family that continue to feed during the winter. In most areas, black crappie provide good cold-weather fishing.

Black Crappie
SCIENTIFIC NAME
Pomoxis nigromaculatus
OTHER COMMON NAMES
speckled perch, papermouth
RANGE & HABITAT
Statewide in clear warmwater lakes, rivers, reservoirs, and sloughs
LENGTH & WEIGHT
To 19+ in. and 4 lb.
LIFESPAN
To 5 years
DIET & SUGGESTED BAIT/LURES
*Feeds on other fish.
Try crappie jigs
or meal worms for bait*

27

White Crappie

to 21 in.

It is possible that all white crappie in California today are the progeny of 16 fish planted in 1917 in a pond near Morena Reservoir, San Diego County. Progeny from this plant were introduced into Morena, Sweetwater, Hodges, Upper Otay, Lower Otay, Murray, Lindo, Grossmont, and Wohlford reservoirs in San Diego County. It wasn't until 1951 that white crappie were successfully introduced into waters north of the Tehachapi Mountains. They are common in Clear Lake, Lake County, and in the sloughs of the Sacramento River, Yolo County.

Distinguishing Characteristics

Silvery white, with dark green or black mottling in the form of vertical bars on sides. These bars are often indistinct in adult fish. Length of dorsal fin base less than the distance from front of dorsal fin to eye. Six dorsal spines.

Life History & Other Notes

White crappie are found in the same general habitat as black crappie, however white crappie tolerate turbid water and mud bottoms, and may outnumber black crappie in this type of habitat. Adult white crappie are fish-eaters. They need abundant forage fish coupled with heavy fishing to provide and maintain a desirable fishery. Without heavy fishing, they tend to overpopulate an area and become stunted. White crappie grow a little faster than black crappie, but both reach the same general size.

Look for white crappie to gather in the shelter of submerged stumps and brush heaps during May or June.

White Crappie

SCIENTIFIC NAME
Pomonis annularis

OTHER COMMON NAMES
silver bass, goggle-eye, silver crappie

RANGE & HABITAT
Statewide in warmwater lakes, rivers, reservoirs and sloughs

LENGTH & WEIGHT
To 21 in. and 4+ lb.

LIFESPAN
To 10 years

DIET & SUGGESTED BAIT/LURES
Feeds on other fish. Try crappie jigs or meal worms for bait

Sacramento Perch

J. Taylor

├──────── *to 12+ in.* ──────┤

This native of California, formerly widespread and numerous, has been eliminated over much of its original range, presumably as a result of the importation of non-native species. It now plays a minor part in the state's sport fisheries. This perch was originally abundant in all the sloughs and slow-flowing channels of the Sacramento-San Joaquin system, and the Pajaro and Salinas rivers as well; now it is seen infrequently in those areas. It has been introduced into artificial impoundments with some success and now is a contributor to the sport fisheries of Lake Almanor, Plumas County; Crowley Lake, Mono County; and San Luis Reservoir, Merced County.

Distinguishing Characteristics

Twelve or thirteen dorsal fin spines differentiate this species from all other members of the sunfish family in California, which have ten or less. Coloration is blackish above, with seven vertical bars, irregular in form and position.

Life History & Other Notes

Sacramento perch are built for life in the waters of the Central Valley floor. They are more tolerant of muddy water, higher temperatures, higher salinities, and higher alkalinities than most other sunfishes. They grow faster and larger in length; however, individuals over 12 in. are rare. They are not extremely active or aggressive, and they do not school. This species is more difficult to catch than introduced sunfishes, but for edibility it ranks among the best.

Sacramento Perch

SCIENTIFIC NAME
Archoplites interruptus

RANGE & HABITAT
Central California rivers, sloughs, lakes and reservoirs

LENGTH & WEIGHT
To 12+ in. and 3+ lb.

LIFESPAN
To 6 years

DIET & SUGGESTED BAIT/LURES
Feeds on insects, crustaceans, small fish. Try crappie jigs and small plastic grubs, or red worms for bait

---

29

Tule Perch

to 8 in.

J. Tomelleri

The tule perch, a

California native, is currently found in the Sacramento River system, Clear Lake, Blue Lakes, Silverwood Lake, and the Russian River, having evidently gone extinct in the Pajaro, Salinas, and much of the San Joaquin river drainage. Three sub-species have been identified in four separate areas: the Sacramento River; Silverwood Lake; Clear Lake and the two nearby Blue Lakes, and the Russian River. Tule perch in the Russian River are only found in the river and its lower tributaries, and *is currently a species of concern which should not be targeted by anglers*. Tule perch generally prefer warmwater lakes, sloughs, streams and rivers.

Distinguishing Characteristics

Deep-bodied, with a definite hump between the head and the dorsal fin. Color variable; back may be light blue or purple, with lighter belly. Sides may have irregular bars; pattern varies with location. Dorsal fin has notable ridge of scales running along base.

Life History & Other Notes

Tule perch eat small invertebrates found on the bottom or floating in mid-water. This perch is the only genus of its family (Embiotocidae, the surfperches) to inhabit fresh water in California. Tule perch, like all surfperches, are livebearers. Female tule perch bear 20 to 90 young, which stay hidden in areas of slow water flow with plenty of plant cover. Young males are able to reproduce a few months after birth.

Tule Perch

SCIENTIFIC NAME
Hysterocarpus traskii

RANGE & HABITAT
*Clear Lake, Blue Lakes,
Lake Silverwood,
Sacramento River
and its tributaries*

LENGTH & WEIGHT
To 8 in. and ~¼ lb.

LIFESPAN
To 7 years

DIET & SUGGESTED BAIT
*Feeds on small invertebrates.
Try red worms for bait*

Yellow Perch

to 12 in.

The yellow perch was introduced in 1891 into Lake Cuyamaca, San Diego County and into the Feather River, Butte County, from Illinois stock. The plant in Lake Cuyamaca did not take; none of the fish survived. Several subsequent importations were made, and by 1918 it was widely distributed, although not numerous, in the Central Valley. Presently it is seldom taken anywhere in this drainage. In 1946 it was discovered in the Klamath River, apparently having migrated there from Oregon. It is now abundant in Iron Gate and Copco Lakes, Siskiyou County, and in the backwaters along the Klamath River.

Distinguishing Characteristics

Body yellow or olive, with 6 to 8 dark vertical bands. Usually does not exceed 12 in.

Life History & Other Notes

In its native range, the yellow perch frequently inhabits trout waters. It lives in lakes, ponds, and the quieter parts of streams. Yellow perch spawn in the spring when water temperatures reach 45° to 55° F. Eggs are laid in ribbons, which are often draped over twigs, stones, and aquatic plants.

Yellow perch often become stunted in small lakes. The Department has no plans to expand their present range.

Yellow Perch

SCIENTIFIC NAME
Perca flavescens

OTHER COMMON NAMES
perch, lake perch

RANGE & HABITAT
Northern California lakes and rivers, rarely in the Central Valley

LENGTH & WEIGHT
To 12 in. and 1 lb.

LIFESPAN
To 5 years

DIET & SUGGESTED BAIT/LURES
Feeds on aquatic insect larvae, snails, crustaceans. Try red worms or night crawlers for bait, or crappie jigs

---

31

Bluegill

— to 15+ in. —

The bluegill is the most abundant sunfish in California. It was first introduced in 1895 in the Bolsa Chica River, Orange County, and Elsinore Lake, Riverside County, but apparently did not survive. In 1908, bluegill from Meredosia, Illinois were sucessfully planted in various waters from Placer County in the north to Orange County in the south.

Distinguishing Characteristics

Dark spot at rear base of dorsal fin, vertical bars on sides, body very deep and compressed, mouth small, gill cover lobe flexible, pectoral fins long and pointed. The Department has conducted studies on Florida bluegill since 1976. They are a discrete sub-species that exhibits a reddish fin coloration, but are difficult to distinguish from the common form.

Life History & Other Notes

Bluegills thrive at water temperatures between 60° and 80° F and generally reach lengths of 4 to 5 in. by the end of their third year. Adults are typically only 6 to 7 in. long, however a 15½ in. bluegill was taken from Ketona Lake,

Alabama. Bluegills are quite prolific and can spawn four times a year in Southern California where high water temperatures are sustained.

Bluegills generally school near some type of cover. They have often been planted with largemouth bass as forage for the bass, as well as to provide a supplemental fishery. The bluegill's schooling behavior often makes for fast and furious sport fishing. They are excellent eating, their flesh being firm, sweet and not too oily.

Bluegill

SCIENTIFIC NAME
Lepomis macrochirus

OTHER COMMON NAMES
sunfish, blue bream

RANGE & HABITAT
Statewide in warmwater lakes and warm, slow-moving streams

LENGTH & WEIGHT
To 15+ in. and 4+ pound.

LIFESPAN
To 11 years

DIET & SUGGESTED BAIT/LURES
Feeds on aquatic insects, snails, small fish, and crayfish. Try red worms or meal worms for bait, or crappie jigs

32

Pumpkinseed

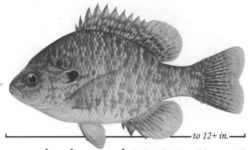

—— to 12+ in. ——

The origin of California populations of pumpkinseed is unknown, but t may be have been introduced to the state as early as 1908. In 1942, pumpkinseed were discovered n the lower Susan River, Lassen County. They are now also found n nearby Honey Lake and in the upper Klamath River; in Iron Gate and Copco lakes, Siskiyou County; n Antelope Creek, a tributary of Lost River, Modoc County; in Lake Davis, Plumas County; in Mountain Meadows Reservoir, Lassen County; in Big Bear Lake, San Bernardino County, and in Hemet Lake, Riverside County. Pumpkinseed prefer clear waters over bottoms of sand or mud and dense aquatic vegetation. They are adapted to cooler waters, especially those with large seasonal fluctuations in temperature.

Distinguishing Characteristics

Gill cover lobe with a spot of orange or red on lower part; cheeks with prominent blue and orange stripes.

Life History & Other Notes

Like redear sunfish, pumpkinseed mainly feed on hard-shelled invertebrates, especially snails and aquatic insects. Spawning begins in May or June when temperatures reach 68° F. Pumpkinseed hybridize easily with other sunfishes, especially bluegill and green sunfish. They grow slowly, perhaps because they live in cooler waters. They are prolific, and stunted populations are not uncommon. The largest fish rarely exceed 12 in.

Pumpkinseed

SCIENTIFIC NAME
Lepomis gibbosus

OTHER COMMON NAMES
yellow sunfish, bream, punky

RANGE & HABITAT
Principally in isolated reservoirs (see above) in clear, cool water over sand or mud bottom with dense vegetation, but may occur statewide

LENGTH & WEIGHT
To 12+ in. and 1 lb.

LIFESPAN
To ~12 years

DIET & SUGGESTED BAIT
Feeds on snails, aquatic insects. Try meal worms or red worms for bait

33

Green Sunfish

to 7 in.

Green sunfish are found in most of California's lakes and slow-moving streams. They are usually not abundant except in mid-elevation lakes and streams that do not contain bluegill or redear sunfish. Green sunfish were first introduced accidentally into Lake Cuyamaca, San Diego County, in 1891 from Illinois stock.

This sunfish is very adaptable and is capable of colonizing disturbed habitats more easily than many other species. They are frequently found in low numbers in the same waters as bluegill, and are often associates of smallmouth bass in small streams. They are also found in some trout lakes. Their temperature tolerance range is large; some green sunfish are able to withstand water temperatures over 97° F.

Distinguishing Characteristics

Mouth relatively large for a sunfish. Body rather bass-shaped; not as deep as bluegill or redear sunfish. Turquoise mottling, often in the form of bars, radiates backwards from snout to eye. Pectoral fins short and rounded.

Life History & Other Notes

Green sunfish begin spawning when temperatures exceed 66° F; nests can be found in shallow waters, either singly or in colonies. They feed primarily on aquatic insects and small fish.

Green sunfish tend to overpopulate a water body and become stunted; even under good growing conditions they seldom exceed 7 in.

Green Sunfish

SCIENTIFIC NAME
Lepomis cyanellus
OTHER COMMON NAMES
shade perch, black perch, slicks
RANGE & HABITAT
*Statewide in lakes and
slow-moving streams*
LENGTH & WEIGHT
To 7 in. and ¼ lb.
LIFESPAN
To 10 years

DIET & SUGGESTED BAIT
*Feeds on aquatic insects
and small fish. Try red worms
or meal worms for bait*

Redear Sunfish

← to 12 in. →

In 1948, redear sunfish

were planted in the Headgate Rock Dam area of the lower Colorado River, San Bernardino County. Since that time, they have been introduced successfully into many areas of the state. They prefer deeper waters of quiet, warm lakes, ponds, and sloughs with dense vegetation.

Distinguishing Characteristics

Gill cover lobe stiff, with broad red or orange margin below and behind. Gill rakers short and stout. Pectoral fins long and pointed.

Life History & Other Notes

Redear sunfish are bottom feeders, eating snails, clams and other invertebrates with shells. They can spawn several times a year beginning when water temperatures reach around 75° F. Redear sunfish generally grow to between 4½ in. and 9 in. long, with a maximum size in California of 12 in.

Redear sunfish are a popular component of warmwater fisheries in California. They grow more rapidly than most other sunfishes and are not as prone to overpopulate and become stunted as the bluegill and green sunfish. Bluegill-redear sunfish hybrids are common in waters where they coexist.

Redear Sunfish

SCIENTIFIC NAME
Lepomis microlophus

OTHER COMMON NAMES
shellcracker, stumpknocker

RANGE & HABITAT
Statewide in deeper waters of warmwater lakes, ponds, and sloughs with dense vegetation

WEIGHT
To 5+ lb.

LIFESPAN
To 7 years

DIET & SUGGESTED BAIT/LURES
Feeds on snails, clams & other invertebrates. Try red worms or meal worms for bait, or crappie jigs

---

35

Warmouth

to 10 in.

Warmouth are fairly

common in parts of the Central Valley and in waters of the Delta, especially near Turlock. They were first planted in 1891 in Lake Cuyamaca, San Diego County, and in the Feather River near Gridley; however, only the Feather River plant was successful. In 1963 they were discovered in the Colorado River and more recently have been found in the Delta sloughs and in Lake Amador, Amador County; Lake Hughes, San Diego County; Lake McClure, Merced County; and the San Joaquin River below Millerton Lake, Fresno County. Warmouth prefer warm, muddy, medium-to-shallow waters of ponds and lakes rather than streams. They have been found in some cooler lakes that support trout.

Distinguishing Characteristics

Body coloration yellowish brown, with three or four brownish bars radiating from the eye across the gill cover. Gill cover lobe stiff and black edged in white, never red. The presence of teeth on the tongue distinguishes it from all other sunfishes in California.

Life History & Other Notes

Warmouth feed on insects, small fishes, crustaceans, and snails. Larger individuals will take crayfish. Spawning starts in May or June when water temperatures approach 69° F. Warmouth will hybridize with other sunfishes, such as bluegill. Growth is slow; they rarely reach more than 10 in. long, and large populations frequently become stunted. They are considered a good-eating sport fish.

Warmouth

SCIENTIFIC NAME
Lepomis gulosus

OTHER COMMON NAMES
warmouth bass, warmouth perch

RANGE & HABITAT
Central and Southern California warmwater lakes, ponds and streams

LENGTH & WEIGHT
To 10 in. and 1 lb.

LIFESPAN
To 8 years

DIET & SUGGESTED BAIT/LURES
*Feeds on insects, small fish, snails, crustaceans.
Try meal worms or red worms for bait, or use crappie jigs*

Tilapia

J. Tomelleri

to ~16 in.

Tilapia were introduced into the irrigation canals and drainage ditches adjacent to the Lower Colorado River in the late 1960s and early 1970s. These fish were planted by the local irrigation district authorities to provide biological control for noxious aquatic plants and insects. Originally, only pure strain fish were stocked. These included blue tilapia (*Tilapia aurea*), Mozambique tilapia (*T. mossambica*), black tilapia (*T. nilotica*), redbelly tilapia (*T. zillii*) and zanzibar tilapia (*T. hornorum*). Today, tilapia found in this region are most likely an interbred mix from the original stock and over 35 years of hybridization. Physical variation seen amongst individual fish is likely caused by a more dominant strain of one of the original species planted in the area.

Tilapia are generally found in shallow, inshore waters, especially in sheltered bays. They are quite common off muddy shores where there is abundant vegetation.

Mozambique Tilapia

In 1964, the first verified free-living population of this species in California was found near the Hot Mineral Spa just east of the Salton Sea. Four years later large populations were found in the Bard Valley near Winterhaven, Imperial County. The source of these two groups is not certain, but the Bard Valley group probably originated from tilapia stocked by the Arizona Game and Fish Department in several drains near Yuma, Arizona.

Starting in 1970, introduction of Mozambique tilapia by local irrigation districts for the purpose of controlling aquatic weed growth resulted in permanent populations in the irrigation systems of the Imperial, Palo Verde, and Coachella valleys; in the Salton Sea, and in the lower Colorado River near the Mexico border. In 1973, introductions were made in the San Gabriel, Los Angeles, and Santa Ana river drainages. Lake Elsinore in Riverside County also supports an abundant, reproducing population. The Mozambique tilapia normally inhabits fresh water, but it is capable of living and breeding in sea water.

continued on pg. 38

37

Tilapia

Tilapia Hybrids

Tilapia are now permanently established in the Salton Sea and its canals and drains, and are also found in the Colorado River and its backwaters downstream from Parker Dam. The Fish and Game Commission prohibits the importation, transportation, and possession of tilapia except in the six counties of Imperial, Riverside, San Bernardino, San Diego, Orange and Los Angeles in Southern California.

Life History & Other Notes

Tilapia feed principally on the leaves and stems of rooted aquatic plants and their associated algae; invertebrate and fish remains have also been found in their stomachs. Tilapia can tolerate temperatures up to 93° F and extreme salinity, but will die at temperatures below 44° F.

Tilapia

SCIENTIFIC NAMES
Tilapia aurea
T. mossambica
T. nilotica
T. zillii
T. honorum

OTHER COMMON NAMES
red tilapia, redbelly tilapia, blue tilapia

RANGE & HABITAT
Southern California, Salton Sea & Colorado River and its drainages

LENGTH & WEIGHT
To ~16 in. and 4 lb.

LIFESPAN
To 11 years

DIET & SUGGESTED BAIT
Feeds on aquatic plants, aquatic insects and small fish. Try using worms or peas for bait

---

Hybrid tilapia taken from Hodges Drain, Riverside County.

Hybrid tilapia taken from the Salton Sea.

38

Trophy Black Bass Recognition Program

Hankering to catch a trophy-sized bass? You're in the right state! Nineteen of the 25 heftiest largemouth caught worldwide were taken from California waters.

To recognize anglers who land California's monster black bass, the Department created the Trophy Black Bass recognition program as part of the Black Bass Conservation and Management Act of 1980. This program:

🐟 Recognizes the extraordinary accomplishment of landing a trophy bass

🐟 Helps the Department maintain records of trophy bass landings

🐟 Assists Department managers in producing more trophy bass in designated waters

To qualify, bass must meet or exceed the following weight criteria:
**largemouth bass: 10 lb.   smallmouth bass: 6 lb.
spotted bass: 6 lb.**

Two witnesses are required to the weighing and measuring of the fish. The Department will award a certificate of recognition suitable for framing to anglers who catch verified trophy black bass. Anglers who catch and release their trophy bass also receive a California Trophy Bass catch-and-release hat or lapel pin.

If you've successfully caught a trophy black bass, complete and mail a Trophy Black Bass application form along with supporting documentation to the Department. Application forms are available on the Trophy Black Bass Angler Recognition Web site and at all Department offices.For more information about the Trophy Black Bass Angler Recognition Program, call (916) 358-2847 or visit:

www.dfg.ca.gov/fish/Fishing/Recognition/TBB

Coldwater Inland Finfish

*C*alifornia's more than 4,100 lakes and reservoirs and nearly 30,000 miles of streams and rivers provide ample coldwater fishing opportunities throughout the state. Both novice and experienced anglers are challenged in their pursuit of trout and other coldwater fish from California's clear mountain lakes down to streams and rivers emptying into the Pacific.

California has 12 native species, sub-species, or forms of trout. The coastal rainbow trout (including the anadromous form, popularly known as *steelhead*) is the most common and widely recognized of the state's native trout, while the beautifully colored California golden trout is the State Fish. Other native trout include the Lahontan cutthroat, Paiute cutthroat, coastal cutthroat, Eagle Lake rainbow, Kern River rainbow, Little Kern golden, McCloud River redband, Goose Lake redband, and Warner Lakes redband. Anglers are strongly encouraged to catch and release the Little Kern golden, Lahontan cutthroat, and Paiute cutthroat presently listed as "Threatened" under the federal Endangered Species Act. One species, the native bull trout (formerly known as the *Dolly Varden*), is now extinct in the state.

Several species of trout and char have been successfully introduced into California including brown trout, brook and lake trout (actually chars), and kokanee (the landlocked form of sockeye salmon).

California Fishing Passport

To help manage the state's trout fisheries, CDFW operates fourteen trout hatcheries and facilities that annually produce and distribute nearly 16 million trout weighing 4 to 5 million pounds. Trout stocking includes several species, of which rainbow trout is the most common. CDFW stocks fingerling-sized fish (2½ to 4 in.), small fish (6–7 in.), medium-sized fish (10-12 in.), and some larger-sized brood stock or "bonus" trout.

By carefully managing California's trout populations CDFW helps to provide a diversity of angling opportunities for anglers, while regulations assist in the maintenance of self-sustaining populations. Size limits on wild fish help to maximize the numbers of larger fish available to anglers, while hatchery trout provide even more recreational angling opportunities. CDFW also aims to increase recreational opportunities in areas of high demand, to meet the needs of all California anglers.

R. Ballanti

Rainbow Trout

Onchorynchus mykiss

The rainbow trout is found throughout California. Since this is the fish most commonly raised in California trout hatcheries, it has been planted in just about every suitable water across the state.

The *coastal* rainbow trout is one of 11 California Heritage Trout species (see pg. 56). This native trout's historic range includes coastal streams statewide, and the Sacramento and San Joaquin River drainages below natural fish migration barriers.

Distinguishing Characteristics

Black spots of various size, from pin points to about one-eighth inch in diameter, but rarely large or perfectly round. Spots on the upper half of head, body, and on dorsal and tail fins. Lateral band reddish to violet, extending from head to tail. Lower side of the head commonly reddish. There are usually no "cutthroat" dashes of red on the membrane beneath the jaw although some rainbow trout in some areas may show small orange marks similar to those of a cutthroat trout. No small red spots on sides or wavy marks or bars on back or dorsal fin.

All trout vary somewhat in their coloration, but the rainbow is extremely variable. Rainbow trout in some lakes and reservoirs may be quite silvery except on the back; they may have very few spots and these may be indistinct, and the red on the head and sides may be completely lacking.

This species may be represented in the lower portions of coastal streams by sea-run rainbow trout (see right) and in the headwaters by resident fish. In some streams the ranges of the two overlap. Rainbow trout of one sub-species will hybridize with other sub-species and with cutthroat trout when their ranges are not separated by some barrier.

Heritage Rainbow Trout Sub-Species

Eagle Lake Rainbow Trout

The native drainage for this sub-species of rainbow trout is Eagle Lake (only fish caught from Eagle Lake will qualify for the Heritage Trout Challenge.).

Onchorynchus mykiss aquilar

This trout may have very few black spots on the head. The middle of the back from the head to the dorsal fin is without spots. The dorsal and tail fins and the upper part of the body have large rounded or elongated spots.

Pine Creek is the only tributary where this trout naturally spawns. With falling lake levels making the creek more inaccessible to trout, the Department developed a hatchery program at Crystal Lake to bolster populations.

Life History & Other Notes

Resident rainbow trout rarely attain large sizes in California. However, in a few of the larger reservoirs and lakes, rainbow trout do grow rapidly (for example, an 18 lb. rainbow trout was recorded from Lake Almanor).

Wild rainbow trout generally spawn in the spring from February through June. Some strains of domesticated hatchery trout have been bred to spawn in the fall, so that their offspring will be larger at planting time.

Coastal rainbow trout are the most abundant and widespread of our native trout, occupying thousands of miles of California streams. Anglers attempting the Heritage Trout Challenge should note that rainbow trout caught outside of historic ranges will not qualify.

Sea-run Rainbow Trout
known as 'Steelhead'

Sea-run rainbow trout, popularly known as *steelhead*, exist in the lower portions of many coastal streams. Sea-run rainbow trout grow larger than resident rainbow trout because they spend one or more years in the ocean under conditions much more favorable to rapid growth.

Sea-run rainbow trout may be found in most coastal and central valley streams, however some populations are protected by the Endangered Species Act. Anglers should review current angling regulations and/or closures for this trout.

Adult sea-run rainbow trout returning to spawn are typically bright, silvery fish with few spots along the back and on the dorsal and tail fins. After residing in a stream for a few weeks, their coloration darkens, the spotting becomes much more profuse, and the sides of the head and the lateral band often turns bright red. They rarely ascend to the headwaters, where resident rainbow trout are found.

Onchorynchus mykiss gilberti

Kern River Rainbow Trout

The native drainage for this sub-species of rainbow trout is the upper main stem (North Fork) of the Kern River and tributaries below natural fish migration barriers (only fish caught from this drainage will qualify for the Heritage Trout Challenge.)

Hybridization with stocked non-native rainbow and golden trout in the Kern River drainage may have altered the Kern River rainbow's historic character through nearly all of its range. Wild trout from the roadside parts of the Kern River are most likely hybridized with introduced trout. Future genetic studies will improve our understanding of this beautiful native trout.

Brown Trout

— to 30 in. —

Although the brown trout is widely scattered throughout California, the waters in which it is abundant are relatively few. In years past, this species was planted in a large part of all the trout waters of the state, but in recent years only a few select lakes and streams have been stocked with brown trout. However, a few of the progeny from earlier plants can still be found, and in a many streams along both sides of the Sierras the "browns" spawn quite successfully.

Distinguishing Characteristics

Coloration variable; usually dark brown or olive brown on the back, shading to golden brown on the sides and white or yellow on the belly. Relatively large, dark spots distinct on the head, body and dorsal fin. No wavy markings on the back or dorsal fin. Red spots surrounded by light halos on the lower sides. This is the only trout with both black and red spots on its body.

Brown trout from lakes may be very pale, almost silvery, on their sides and belly. "Sea-run" brown trout returning to certain rivers from the ocean are silvery, resembling sea-run rainbow trout, and may be without red spots.

Life History & Other Notes

The brown trout is characteristically wary, and those who can catch it rate it as a "fisherman's fish." Many different forms of brown trout were historically stocked in California, which has led to the vast array of color and spotting patterns that anglers often encounter. Brown trout spawn in the fall and often are easier to catch during this period.

Brown Trout

SCIENTIFIC NAME
Salmo trutta

OTHER COMMON NAMES
browns, brownie

RANGE & HABITAT
Coldwater lakes, reservoirs & streams throughout California

LENGTH & WEIGHT
Small streams: To 15 in.
Lakes: To 30 in. and 20 lb.

LIFESPAN
Smaller streams: To 7 years
Larger streams & lakes: To 12 years

DIET & SUGGESTED BAIT/LURES
Eats insects, fish. Try bait, flies spinners, plugs

Brook Trout

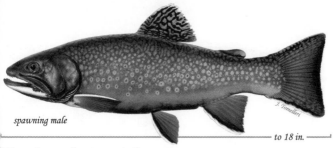

spawning male

to 18 in.

The brook trout has been scattered by hatchery planting from the San Bernardino Mountains of Southern California northward to the Oregon border. Many State waters have been planted with this species, but it hasn't become well established except in high mountain lakes and in the small streams of mountain meadows. It doesn't do very well in California waters lying much below 4,000 ft. elevations, and is found more commonly between 5,000 and 9,000 ft.

Distinguishing Characteristics

Back and sides usually dark olive green, with large and nearly round lighter spots on sides. The spots become wavy lines on the back, which are characteristic of this trout. Dorsal fin has dark wavy lines, no spots. Usually red spots on sides, may be missing in brook trout from lakes. Ventral and anal fins usually with distinct white borders along anterior margins. Males show considerable orange-red on the belly at breeding time.

Life History & Other Notes

The brook trout can spawn not only in stream environments but also in lake-bottom springs or along lake shores. After initial stocking efforts, most California high-country lakes can maintain a naturally reproducing population of brook trout. Brook trout do not grow as large in California as they do in some parts of the eastern U.S., but many concede that pan-sized brook trout from our high-mountain lakes can have the finest flavor of all California trout.

Brook Trout

SCIENTIFIC NAME
Salvelinus fontinalis

OTHER COMMON NAMES
brookie

RANGE & HABITAT
Statewide in high mountain lakes and small streams

LENGTH & WEIGHT
To 18 in. and 5 lbs.

LIFESPAN
Small streams: To 4 years
Larger streams & small lakes:
To 11 years

DIET & SUGGESTED BAIT/LURES
Eats small aquatic insects, fish.
Try small flies, spinners

45

Lake Trout

to 30 in.

The lake trout, or *mackinaw* as it is often called in California, was brought to this state from Michigan in 1894. It has not been widely distributed because of its tendency to feed upon other trout, and is sometimes blamed for the disappearance of the Lahontan cutthroat trout from Lake Tahoe. Self-sustaining populations of lake trout are present in Lake Tahoe, Fallen Leaf Lake, Stony Ridge Lake, and Donner Lake, all of which are in the Truckee River drainage. Lake trout have recently been introduced into other waters as well.

Distinguishing Characteristics
Background color on body usually dark gray, but varies from pale gray to almost black. Entire body except for belly covered with large pale spots. Tail fin deeply forked. Head is pointed and body is relatively slender.

Life History & Other Notes
This trout tends to live in the deeper parts of lakes and is usually caught by trolling with wire line, to which large spinners and frequently minnows are attached. It commonly feeds upon other fish and grows to large sizes; a 15 lb. lake trout is not uncommon. This is the only trout which does not construct some sort of nest or cover its eggs with gravel. Its eggs are dropped into the loose rocks or ledges and shelves on the lake bottom.

This trout was originally described in 1792 by Johann Walbaum from fish taken in Hudson Bay. Its scientific name was taken from the Native American name for this fish, *namaycush*.

Lake Trout
SCIENTIFIC NAME
Salvelinus namaycush

OTHER COMMON NAMES
mackinaw

RANGE & HABITAT
Northern Sierra Nevada lakes

LENGTH & WEIGHT
Average 30 in. & 15 lbs.

LIFESPAN
To 25 years

DIET & SUGGESTED BAIT/LURES
*Feeds on other fish.
Try trolling a spinner
with a minnow
on a wire line*

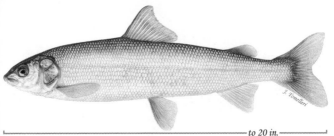

to 20 in.

The mountain whitefish is found throughout the streams and lakes of the eastern slope of the Sierra Nevada, but is most common in the Truckee and Carson rivers.

Distinguishing Characteristics

Sides silvery, back and fins light brown. The small mouth superficially resembles that of a sucker. Mountain whitefish can be immediately distinguished from suckers by the presence of an adipose fin, one indication of their ties with the trout and salmon.

Life History & Other Notes

Mountain whitefish are often taken by trout anglers, since they are found in the same waters as trout and eat much the same food. Many anglers have discarded them as suckers or as inedible fish. Neither of these assumptions is correct. Mountain whitefish are as good to eat as trout and are not at all hard to distinguish from suckers if one remembers to look for the adipose fin [see pg. 11 for description of adipose fin]. Ironically, a true sucker of the Truckee River develops a red stripe on its sides and is often taken home as a rainbow trout by anglers who would throw away mountain whitefish.

Mountain whitefish spawn in the fall in the gravel of stream riffles. The eggs develop in the stream during the winter and take about five months to hatch at 35° F.

Mountain whitefish may be taken by anglers only during trout season. Generally, the same regulations apply. We hope that their inclusion here will identify them to more anglers and prevent waste of this fine game fish.

Mountain Whitefish

SCIENTIFIC NAME
Prosopium williamsoni

RANGE & HABITAT
Eastern slope of the Sierra Nevada in lakes and streams

LENGTH
To 20 in.

LIFESPAN
To 10 years

DIET & SUGGESTED BAIT/LURES
Eats insects, insect larvae & nymphs Artificial flies or bait fished on or near the bottom work well

47

Kokanee Salmon

spawning male

to 20 in.

Kokanee have been planted in numerous lakes in California since their initial introduction in 1941 and have established self perpetuating populations in several waters, including some 'stunted' populations, such as in Trinity Lake which contains only small fish. Fishery managers may choose to adjust annual stocking allotments to adjust the size of fish in some waters.

Distinguishing Characteristics

Back dark blue, sides silvery, with forked tail. In the fall as spawning season approaches, the bodies of both male and female kokanee turn a deep red, while the head and tail remain olive green. The lower jaw of the spawning male develops the characteristic hook common to Pacific salmon. Rays in anal fin 13 to 17 (usually 14 to 15) as opposed to 9 to 12 (rarely 13) in trout.

Life History & Other Notes

Kokanee belong to the same scientific family as the trout, and prefer the same cool waters. They are primarily plankton feeders, preferring the open water areas of lakes. Kokanee compete with small trout for food, but can provide forage for large lake trout.

Mature kokanee ascend streams or gather over gravel bars in lakes in the fall to spawn. Kokanee are the landlocked form of sockeye salmon and, like their ocean-going relatives, die after spawning.

Kokanee can be caught with flies, bait or lures. When trolling, a rubber band between line and leader prevents the hook from tearing their soft mouths.

Kokanee Salmon

SCIENTIFIC NAME
Oncorhynchus nerka

OTHER COMMON NAMES
Little redfish, blueback, silver trout

RANGE & HABITAT
Northern and central California lakes and reservoirs

LENGTH & WEIGHT
To 20 in. and 4+ lb.

LIFESPAN
To 4 years

DIET & SUGGESTED BAIT/LURES
*Feeds on plankton; may be caught on flies, bait or lures.
Most are caught by trolling lures on downriggers*

California
Heritage
Trout

J. Tomelleri

—— to 18 in. ——

The California golden trout is the freshwater State Fish of California, and one of 11 California Heritage Trout species. This native trout's historic range includes the South Fork Kern River drainage and Golden Trout Creek drainage from about 6,300 to 10,500 ft. elevations.

Distinguishing Characteristics

Yellow and red on lower sides and belly. Cheeks and gill cover often red, as are the pectoral, ventral and anal fins. Dorsal and anal fins usually with white tips, sometimes bordered with black. The spotting can be distinctive, with relatively few round, black spots on back and dorsal fin, but there is a great deal of spotting variation. Parr marks (larger olive spots along lateral line) distinct on young fish and adults alike.

A greater number of black spots, and especially the presence of spots below the lateral line, distinguishes this trout from the Little Kern golden trout.

Life History & Other Notes

The extremely vibrant coloration of this trout resulted in its being named the offical freshwater State Fish. California golden trout have been stocked extensively in lakes and streams between Kings Canyon and Yosemite National Parks, but golden trout from these waters do not qualify for the Heritage Trout Challenge. Also, Cottonwood Lakes and Cottonwood Creek, although designated Wild Trout waters, are in the Owens River basin which is not a historic golden trout drainage; thus, golden trout caught in these waters will not qualify for the Heritage Trout Challenge.

California Golden Trout

SCIENTIFIC NAME
Oncorhynchus mykiss aguabonita
OTHER COMMON NAMES
Volcano Creek golden trout
RANGE & HABITAT
Native: South Fork Kern River, Golden Trout Creek. Transplanted in lakes & streams throughout the central Sierra Nevada
LENGTH & WEIGHT
Small streams: to 12 in.
Lakes: to 18 in.
LIFESPAN
To 9 years
DIET
Eats insects, insect larvae & nymphs

49

Coastal Cutthroat Trout

California Heritage Trout

J. Tomelleri

— to 20 in. —

The coastal cutthroat trout is one of 11 California Heritage Trout species. This trout is found in the lower courses of most coastal streams from the Eel River northward. It is not generally abundant and seems to have difficulty competing with rainbow trout. Limited numbers of sea-run cutthroat occur in these streams, but are somewhat difficult to distinguish from sea-run rainbows and so are often overlooked.

Distinguishing Characteristics

Back usually dark olive green. Sides much lighter, belly silvery white. Usually a pair of red streaks ("cutthroat" marks) present on the membrane between the jawbones. Body and all fins usually covered with large, irregular black spots. Spotting does not extend to the lower sides and belly of all fish.

Life History & Other Notes

The coastal cutthroat is a northern trout whose range extends only a short distance into California. Unlike sea-run rainbow trout, sea-run cutthroat seldom venture long distances in the ocean, usually staying within a few miles of the coast. The Smith River drainage is a stronghold for coastal cutthroat and many are found in large river estuaries like those of the Smith and Klamath rivers and Redwood Creek. Also, coastal lagoons such as Stone Lagoon and Lake Earl have held some large cutthroat trout.

The coastal cutthroat trout was originally described in 1836 by Sir John Richardson from fish caught in the Cathlapootl River in Oregon. Its scientific name honors Capt. William Clark of the Lewis and Clark Expedition.

Coastal Cutthroat Trout

SCIENTIFIC NAME
Oncorhynchus clarkii clarkii

OTHER COMMON NAMES
coastal cutts, cutties

RANGE & HABITAT
Coastal streams from the Eel River northward

LENGTH & WEIGHT
To 20 in. and 5 lb.

LIFESPAN
Small streams: To 5 years
Large rivers: To 7 years

DIET & SUGGESTED BAIT/LURES
Eats insects, small fish
Try flies, spinners

Goose Lake Redband Trout

California Heritage Trout

to ~12 in.

Goose Lake redband trout are one of 11 California Heritage Trout. This native trout's range includes Goose Lake basin in California and Oregon and its tributaries; upper Pit River and headwater tributaries, and the South Fork Pit River drainage (trout caught from the Pit River system downstream of Bieber do not qualify for the Heritage Trout Challenge). Although redband trout can grow to large size in Goose Lake, they are seldom caught there.

Smaller-sized Goose Lake redband trout are usually easier to find in the tributary streams and headwaters of the Pit River.

Distinguishing Characteristics
Spotting and coloration similar to coastal rainbow trout, with subtle differences. Redband trout usually have a definitive red band that runs along the lateral line. They're almost always profusely spotted, with larger spots dominating the area near the base of the tail. Small purplish parr marks are retained through adulthood in most stream populations. Fins usually orange with white tips on the dorsal, anal, and pelvic fins. Lake populations are less spotted and the colors more muted.

Life History & Other Notes
In years with plentiful rainfall and good water conditions, Goose Lake can provide a productive environment for fish to grow, and trout migrating into the lake reach larger sizes. During normal to drought conditions the lake is not as conducive to the trout's growth, and the fishery becomes more dependent on the handful of tributaries that provide habitat for the resident fish.

Goose Lake Redband Trout

SCIENTIFIC NAME
Oncorhynchus mykiss subspecies

OTHER COMMON NAMES
redband

RANGE & HABITAT
Native to Goose Lake basin, upper Pit River and headwater tributaries, and South Fork Pit River drainage

LENGTH & WEIGHT
Small streams: to 12 in.
Some larger fish in lakes

LIFESPAN
To 5 years

DIET
Eats insects, insect larvae & nymphs

51

Lahontan Cutthroat Trout

California Heritage Trout

stream resident

J. Tomelleri

to 30 in.

Lahontan cutthroat trout are one of 11 California Heritage Trout. In California, the Lahontan cutthroat trout is a native of the Truckee, Walker, and Carson river drainages and does not occur naturally in waters draining into the Pacific Ocean. This range has been extended somewhat by hatchery planting, however only trout taken from the previously-mentioned river drainages qualify for the Heritage Trout Challenge.

Distinguishing Characteristics

Body usually a dark, yellowish-olive color from back to belly. Sides have a broad, pinkish stripe. Sides of the head often scarlet. Entire body covered with large, black spots. Two distinct red stripes on the membrane beneath the jaw.

Life History & Other Notes

The Lahontan cutthroat is listed as Threatened under the Endangered Species Act, having been eliminated from most of its native range. Recovery efforts in California have established new, wild populations in several streams. Two of these, Slinkard Creek and the Upper Truckee River, a Heritage Trout Water, are open for catch-and-release cutthroat angling. There are also many other lakes and streams in historic drainages that are stocked with Lahontan cutthroat trout from the Heenan Lake broodstock.

The Lahontan cutthroat trout was once called the "Tahoe trout" due to the abundant populations that resided in Lake Tahoe. The lake was fished out in the 1940s due to considerable market demand for "black-spotted trout," which was its market name.

Lahontan Cutthroat Trout

SCIENTIFIC NAME
Oncorhynchus clarkii henshawi

OTHER COMMON NAMES
cutt

RANGE & HABITAT
Trukee, Walker and Carson river drainages

LENGTH & WEIGHT
Small streams: To 12 in.
Lakes: To 30 in. and 12 lb.

LIFESPAN
To 10 years

DIET & SUGGESTED BAIT/LURES
Feeds on insects and small fish. Try spinners and flies

Little Kern Golden Trout

California Heritage Trout

J. Tomelleri

to 12 in.

Little Kern golden

trout are one of 11 California Heritage Trout. This native trout's range includes the Little Kern River drainage above the lowest fish migration barrier upstream of the Forks of the Kern.

Distinguishing Characteristics

The Little Kern golden trout more closely resembles the California golden trout than the Kern River rainbow trout. The Little Kern golden trout may be differentiated from the California golden trout by

its more profuse spotting, and the fact that the underside of the fish is less colorful.

Life History & Other Notes

The Little Kern golden trout may represent an early ancestral line that began when redband trout invaded the Kern drainage. Over time the Little Kern River became isolated from the mainstem through migrational barriers, however biologists speculate that a coastal rainbow trout invasion may have also influenced the development of the Little Kern golden trout.

This trout is listed as Threatened under the Endangered Species Act. Good populations are present in most of the waters in the Little Kern basin within the Golden Trout Wilderness. Many of these streams' fish populations have been restored by CDFW's lengthy recovery efforts. This threatened sub-species of trout was confined to about 10 miles of stream when recovery efforts began in 1975. CDFW's eventual goal is to remove this sub-species from the Endangered Species list. If successful, this will be the only fish removed from the list due to sufficient recovery.

Little Kern Golden Trout

SCIENTIFIC NAME
Oncorhynchus mykiss whitei
RANGE & HABITAT
Little Kern River drainage
LENGTH
To 12 in.
LIFESPAN
To 5 years
DIET & SUGGESTED BAIT/LURES
*Eats insects,
insect larvae & nymphs
Try assorted bait
and flies*

53

McCloud River Redband Trout

California Heritage Trout

— to 20 in. —

The McCloud River redband trout is one of 11 California Heritage Trout. This native trout's historic range includes the McCloud River and tributaries upstream of the Upper Falls.

Distinguishing Characteristics

As with the other redband trout, the McCloud redband trout generally exhibits the spotting and coloration of coastal rainbow trout with some subtle differences. Redband trout usually have a definitive red band that runs along the lateral line (thus the name *redband*). They are usually profusely spotted with larger spots dominating the area near the base of the tail. Small purplish parr marks are retained through adulthood in most stream populations. Fins are usually orange in coloration with white tips on the dorsal, anal, and pelvic fins. Lake populations are less spotted and the colors more muted.

Life History & Other Notes

The McCloud redband trout's ancestors survived the last Ice Age in the upper McCloud drainage east of Mt. Shasta in an area that was spared from glaciers. These redbands were isolated from coastal rainbow trout and bull trout by barrier falls downstream. These trout are relegated to the main stem of the McCloud River and its smaller tributaries, where they are abundant. There is a unique form of redband within the upper McCloud drainage which may be a distinct species; however, currently the stream in which it is found is closed to fishing. Anglers should be aware of current fishing regulations before they fish any of the waters in this drainage.

McCloud River Redband Trout

SCIENTIFIC NAME
Oncorhynchus mykiss stonei

OTHER COMMON NAMES
McCloud redside

RANGE & HABITAT
Native to McCloud River & tributaries upstream of Upper Falls

LENGTH
Small streams: To 12 in.
Larger rivers: To 20 in.

LIFESPAN
To 7 years

DIET & SUGGESTED BAIT/LURES
Eats insects, insect larvae & nymphs
Try assorted bait and flies

Warner Lakes Redband Trout

California Heritage Trout

— to 8 in. —

The Warner Lakes redband trout is one of 11 California Heritage Trout. This native trout's historic range includes tributaries of the Warner Lakes basin in the northeastern corner of California, on the east slope of the Warner Mountains.

Distinguishing Characteristics

As with the other redband trout, the Warner Lakes redband trout generally exhibits the spotting and coloration of coastal rainbow trout with some subtle differences.

Redband trout usually have a definitive red band which runs along the lateral line (thus the name *redband*). They are usually profusely spotted, with larger spots dominating the area near the base of the tail. Small purplish parr marks are retained through adulthood in most stream populations. Fins are usually orange in coloration with white tips on the dorsal, anal, and pelvic fins.

Life History & Other Notes

This is one of the rarest native trout in California, found in just a few streams on the east side of the Warner Mountains in Modoc County. Warner Lakes redband and Goose Lake redband trout are very similar in characteristics and appearance. Anglers attempting the Heritage Trout Challenge should note that the Warner Lakes redband trout is not found in the Warner Valley, a tributary to the North Fork Feather River near Lassen Volcanic National Park, or other "Warner Valleys" in the state. Given the limited distribution of this trout in California, anglers should take extreme care when fishing for them; catch-and-release is highly recommended.

Warner Lakes Redband Trout

SCIENTIFIC NAME
Oncorhynchus mykiss subspecies

RANGE & HABITAT
Tributaries of the Warner Lakes basin, Modoc County

LENGTH & WEIGHT
To 8 in.

LIFESPAN
To 5 years

DIET & SUGGESTED BAIT/LURES
Eats insects, insect larvae & nymphs Due to small size of this trout, use only small lures and flies. Do not use bait (increases risk of death caused by deep hooking)

55

The California Heritage Trout Challenge

Trout have inhabited California waters from the Sierras to the Pacific ocean since prehistoric times. California's native trout include:

- *Coastal rainbow*
- *Eagle Lake rainbow*
- *McCloud River redband*
- *Goose Lake redband*
- *Warner Lakes redband*
- *Kern River rainbow*
- *California golden*
- *Little Kern golden*
- *Coastal cutthroat*
- *Lahontan cutthroat*
- *Paiute cutthroat*

To raise awareness of California's native or "heritage" trout, CDFW developed the Heritage Trout Challenge to tests an angler's ability to catch six different forms of native trout from their historic California drainages. The "Challenge" may take anglers to various locations around the state, from roadside streams to remote areas high in the Sierras.

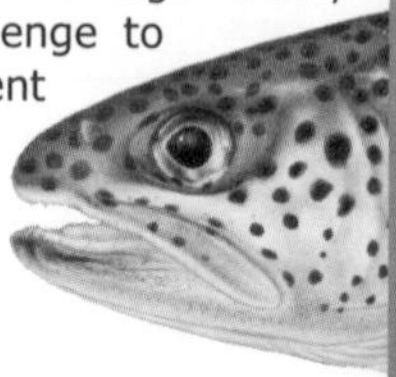

Anglers who are up to the "Challenge" may take as long as they wish to catch the six trout and qualify for this special award: there are no time limits. Native trout caught in the appropriate waters and verified with a photo will qualify, even if caught years ago.

Anglers who successfully meet the "Challenge" will receive a certificate of recognition suitable for framing, illustrated by reknowned artist Joseph Tomelleri.

If you've succeded in catching six California native trout from their historic drainages, complete and mail a Heritage Trout Challenge application form along with supporting documentation to CDFW. Application forms are available at CDFW office or on the Heritage Trout Challenge Web site. For more information, including a list of historic heritage trout drainages, visit the Heritage Trout Challenge Web site at:

www.dfg.ca.gov/fish/Resources/WildTrout

Inland Shellfish

California contains a vast array of inland shellfish including mollusks and crustaceans. Sport fishing regulations provide for the take of two freshwater shellfish: the crayfish and freshwater clams.

Crayfish are harvested both for bait and for human consumption. Signal crayfish, Shasta crayfish, red swamp crayfish, and virile crayfish are the predominant species recognized in California.

The signal crayfish resides in rivers, streams, lakes and reservoirs and is very commonly found in the Sacramento-San Joaquin Delta where it is commercially harvested. Look for them among rocks and aquatic weeds where they may be observed foraging along the bottom.

The red swamp crayfish prefers sloughs, canals, and ditches where the water is relatively warm and vegetation is plentiful, such as the irrigation systems and rice fields of the Central Valley, and in Southern California. Each fall and winter most of these waterways are drained and huge quantities of crayfish are lost. CDFW encourages the use of crayfish and clam resources (for food or bait), but if you plan to venture onto private lands, be sure to get landowner permission.

Red Swamp Crayfish

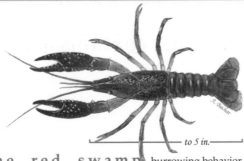

to 5 in.

The red swamp crayfish was introduced to California in the early 1900s from Louisiana. It is now found throughout Southern California and in the heavily agricultural Central Valley. It can also be found in some parts of the Sacramento-San Joaquin Delta, but usually prefers ponds, slower streams and creeks, and irrigation canals in both freshwater and brackish environments.

Distinguishing Characteristics

Usually brick red when adult, juveniles are drab gray. Somewhat smaller than the native variety. Carapace shell and claws covered in bumps. Blue vein visible under the tail. Pincers narrow and long.

Life History & Other Notes

Although it is highly prized in its native Louisiana, this aggressive, territorial crayfish is considered an agricultural pest in California. Unlike signal crayfish, the red swamp crayfish thrives in the rice fields of the Central Valley, making its home by burrowing 24 to 40 inches into the mud banks of the rice checks and levees. They can seriously weaken earthen banks, increasing erosion. This crayfish's burrowing behavior destroys other important wildlife habitat as well.

Red swamp crayfish feed on young rice shoots (taking a further toll on rice crops) and other plants, insect larvae, tadpoles, snails, and newt larvae. They are not affected by newt toxins, which ward off predation by native crayfish. This makes native newts particularly susceptible to predation by this introduced crayfish, and in fact they are blamed for declines in newt populations in some areas.

Red Swamp Crayfish

SCIENTIFIC NAME
Procambarus clarkii

OTHER COMMON NAMES
Louisiana crawdad

RANGE & HABITAT
South & Central California in slower streams & creeks, irrigation canals, rice paddies

LENGTH
To 5 in.

DIET / SUGGESTED BAIT
Feeds on plants, small invertebrates & amphibians Bait traps or lines with liver, bacon, fish, canned cat or dog food

Signal Crayfish

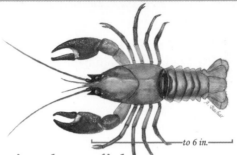

The signal crayfish is a California native found throughout the northern and central parts of the state, and in scattered lakes and reservoirs in Southern California. It occurs in fast, cold streams and rivers, and in the Sacramento-San Joaquin Delta where it is also trapped for commercial export to Sweden.

Distinguishing Characteristics

Generally brownish to greenish in color, with a smooth carapace shell.

Signal Crayfish

SCIENTIFIC NAME
Pacificastacus leniusculus

OTHER COMMON NAMES
crawdads, crayfish

RANGE & HABITAT
Statewide, but most often in central and northern California in cool flowing water in streams, lakes, reservoirs, rivers & river deltas

LENGTH
To 6 in.

SUGGESTED BAIT
Bait traps or lines with liver, bacon, fish, canned cat or dog food

---

White "signal" patches at joints of the large claws.

Life History & Other Notes

Signal crayfish are the largest crayfish in California. They are primarily active at night. Most people use crayfish traps to efficiently harvest this crustacean. Traps are left in the water for at least most of the night. In lakes and reservoirs and in rivers such as the Sacramento River, traps should be set in at least 8 ft. of water off a rocky bank. In smaller rivers and streams, again look for areas of rocks and gravel out of the main current to set a trap.

Unlike the red swamp crayfish (introduced from Louisiana) and other non-native intruders, signal crayfish do not burrow into the ground. The more aggressive red swamp crayfish will usually out-compete the native crayfish for food, thus encroaching on its range. Not much can be done about reducing the numbers of non-native crayfish in areas where they are already well-established, but with a little common sense their further spread can be prevented. Crayfish should never be carried from one body of water to another and released.

59

Anadromous Fishes

*A*nadromous fishes are curiosities of the animal world, beginning their lives in fresh water, then migrating to the ocean to grow and mature, and finally swimming back to fresh water to reproduce. Most people would probably regard them as no more than curiosities if it were not for the most familiar member of the group—the salmonids.

The term anadromous means "up running" and refers to fishes that spend part of their lives in the ocean but move into fresh water to spawn. Different species show differing degrees of anadromous behavior. The most extreme examples migrate from hundreds of miles out at sea to hundreds of miles upriver, while other species only move from brackish water a short distance into fresh water to spawn.

Salmon comes to mind for most people when asked about anadromous fishes. Aside from being fun to catch and very tasty to eat, they are also highly valued by recreational and commercial fishermen. Their spawning runs are well-known events, and in some places crowds gather just to watch them in their upstream journeys to spawn.

In addition to salmon, there are many other important anadromous game fishes living in our rivers, streams, delta and ocean waters, including sturgeon, striped bass, and shad. California's anadromous species are

not only challenging game fish for anglers, but juvenile anadromous fish also serve an important role as forage for other fishes.

California provides many unique fishing opportunities for anadromous fishes. Because of the different waters that they occupy during their life span, these fish are able to exploit the numerous coastal streams and bays along California's coast, especially in the Delta area where the Sacramento and San Joaquin rivers and their tributaries come together, emptying into the vast San Francisco and San Pablo Bay estuary system, and the Pacific Ocean west of the Golden Gate Bridge. No other estuary system like this exists in the entire western United States. Because the Delta and San Francisco-San Pablo Bay estuary system are so large, anadromous fish are generally available to anglers at various geographic locations there throughout the year.

Note: Information about anadromous (sea-run) rainbow trout (aka "steelhead") may be found in the Inland Coldwater Fishes section under rainbow trout.

Chinook Salmon
a courtesy T. Tanaka

American Shad

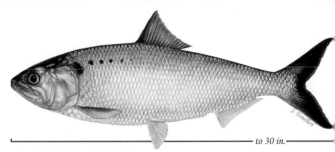

to 30 in.

American shad are native to the Atlantic Coast and are an introduced species to the Pacific coast. They were first planted in the Sacramento River in 1871, with additional plants made for several years thereafter. They did remarkably well: by 1879 American shad were being taken in marketable quantities and by 1880 they had spread as far north as the Columbia River in Washington, where they had also been planted in 1885. American shad may currently be found off the entire coast of California, however they are not common south of Monterey.

In California, American shad have become established in many of the larger streams and rivers from San Francisco north. The greatest numbers are found in the Sacramento River, its delta and major tributaries. They may also be found in the San Joaquin River system, the Russian, Klamath, Trinity, Mokelumne, Stanislaus and Eel rivers, and occasionally in the Smith River. They are highly migratory, and may be found statewide.

Distinguishing Characteristics

Metallic blue along back, side and belly bright silver. Dorsal fin situated at mid-back; ventral fin directly below the dorsal fin, each with a fleshy appendage at its base. No adipose fin. Belly with sharp-edged, saw-toothed scales called "scutes." No lateral line. Row of black spots along the upper front on the sides. Scales are large and easily lost.

American Shad

SCIENTIFIC NAME
Alosa sapidissima

OTHER COMMON NAMES
shad

RANGE & HABITAT
Fisheries exist mostly in freshwater rivers and deltas

LENGTH & WEIGHT
To 30 in. and 7+ lb.

LIFESPAN
To 11 years

DIET & SUGGESTED BAIT/LURES
Feeds on shrimp, small crustaceans & fish. Try fishing with flies and lures such as shad darts, small plastic worms, spinners, or spoons

Life History & Other Notes

American shad belong to the herring family. They are anadromous, although landlocked populations have survived (Millerton Lake, above Friant Dam, contains a reproducing population of American shad).

Young shad feed on small crustaceans and insect larvae while in fresh water; in estuaries they feed on shrimps other crustaceans. Adults feed on shrimps, crustaceans, and small fish. During spawning runs the adults actually eat very little, but like salmon they will still strike at a fly or lure.

Shad spawning runs occur from late April to early July. In many spawning streams, shad go as far upstream as they are able, but unlike salmon, they do very poorly at ascending fish ladders and may be stopped even by a relatively low dam with a fish ladder. Spawning takes place where there is good current in tidal fresh water or farther upstream. Shad are broadcast spawners and do not make nests,

although most spawning occurs over gravel or sand bottoms well above all tidal action. One female may lay from 120,000 to over half a million eggs. American shad sometimes die after spawning, but many travel back to salt water and rejoin oceanic schools.

Shad eggs drift with the current near the bottom, usually hatching in 4 to 6 days, depending on temperature. Some young shad move downstream into brackish water soon after hatching, but large numbers remain in fresh water through November at 5 to 6 months of age. By December, most have left fresh water for the ocean, where they live until they mature at around 3 to 5 years of age.

Fishing for American shad occurs in fresh water. The appeal of this fishery is enhanced by its proximity to centers of population. The extreme example is in Sacramento, where most residents can drive to good shad fishing waters in 10 to 20 minutes. The scientific name for this species, *sapidissima*, means "most delicious."

Striped Bass

to 4 ft.

Striped bass were introduced to California in 1879, when 132 small fish from the Navesink River in New Jersey were released into San Francisco Bay near Martinez. In 1882, three hundred more fish were released into lower Suisun Bay. By 1892 a flourishing commercial fishery had developed, which was subsequently closed in 1935 in an effort to build a sport fishery.

Since their introduction, striped bass have spread north to Canada and south to Mexico. In California, most striped bass are found in the Sacramento-San Joaquin Delta and the larger tributary rivers downstream from dams. Limited fisheries also exist in Tomales Bay and the Russian River, but outside of the aforementioned areas, sea-run striped bass are uncommon.

Landlocked striped bass exist in Black Butte, Camp Far West, Millerton, Modesto, San Antonio, Santa Margarita, and Success reservoirs, Lake Mendocino, and the Colorado River system. Striped bass are also present in the federal Central Valley Project, State Water Project, and the Contra Costa County canals and reservoirs using the Sacramento-San Joaquin Delta as a source.

Distinguishing Characteristics

Silvery with seven or eight conspicuous horizontal blackish stripes on the back and sides (one is the lateral line). Eyes small. Body is slender and not noticeably compressed (flattened side to side). Pectoral fins relatively short, not reaching past the tips of the ventral fins.

Striped Bass

SCIENTIFIC NAME
Morone saxitilis

OTHER COMMON NAMES
stripers

RANGE & HABITAT
San Francisco Bay, Sacramento-San Joaquin Delta, larger rivers and some lakes and reservoirs

LENGTH & WEIGHT
To 4 ft. and 90 lb.

LIFESPAN
To 20+ years, average to 10 years

DIET/SUGGESTED BAIT
Feeds on fishes and shrimp. Try using sardines, bloodworms, pile worms, or ghost shrimp for bait, or artificial lures

Life History & Other Notes

Striped bass are members of the temperate bass family. They appear to depend rather strongly on an anadromous existence. Although landlocked populations exist in California, many of these groups are not self-reproducing. Landlocked striped bass succeed in breeding only when there are rivers long enough and with sufficient flow to keep the eggs suspended until they hatch (about two days, depending on temperature).

Adult sea-run striped bass begin moving into fresh water in October and November. Spawning commences in the spring when the water temperature reaches 58° F. These bass spawn from April through mid-June, when they begin moving out to salt water again.

Striped bass are very prolific. A 5-pound female may spawn 180,000 eggs in one season and a 15-pound female is capable of producing over a million eggs.

Striped bass are broadcast spawners that gather in large groups at the surface to reproduce. Spawning occurs in moderate to swift currents, where the transparent eggs drift suspended in the water until they hatch. The young swim or drift downstream to estuarine nursery areas and eventually make their way out to sea.

Striped bass are fast growing fish. They are only about 1/6 in. long at hatching and grow to 4 in. at one year, 10 inches at two years, 16 inches at three years, and 20 inches at four years.

In the winter months, striped bass are scattered in both fresh and salt water but do not bite well until the water begins to warm in the spring.

Fish move upriver in the spring to spawn. During the summer, fishing is usually best in San Francisco Bay, especially near Treasure Island, Alcatraz Island, Raccoon Strait, and near the south tower of the Golden Gate Bridge. Though summer fishing usually continues to be best in San Francisco Bay, however there are also good fishing opportunities in the Sacramento and San Joaquin rivers and their tributaries, as well as the Sacramento-San Joaquin Delta.

Anglers pursuing striped bass use shiner perch, anchovies, sardines, bloodworms, pile worms, and shrimp for bait. Striped bass will also take a wide range of artificial lures, including flies.

Chinook Salmon

— to 4+ ft. —

Chinook salmon are native to California. All members of this family require cool or cold water. Prolonged temperatures of higher than 70° F are usually detrimental to this fish, while temperatures over 80° F are often lethal.

In the ocean, Chinook salmon are found statewide but they are most abundant from Monterey northwards. Once they enter fresh water to spawn, they can be found in some astonishingly small tributaries. California's largest spawning populations are in the Sacramento-San Joaquin River system. Chinook salmon were also historically abundant in the Klamath, Eel and Smith river systems. Smaller runs occur in Redwood Creek, Mad River, Mattole River, and some other coastal streams. Landlocked Chinook salmon may be found in the following lakes: Shasta, Berryessa, Almanor, Folsom, Spaulding, Del Valle, Isabella, McClure, Don Pedro, and Pine Flat.

Distinguishing Characteristics

Prominent adipose fin. Ventral fins are abdominal with a scaly, fleshy appendage at the base of each. All rays of the dorsal fin soft. Lateral line prominent. Scales small.

At sea: Bluish to gray on the back, silvery on the sides and belly. Numerous black spots on back, dorsal fin, and usually on both lobes of the tail fin (coho salmon have no spots on the lower lobe of the tail fin). Spots on the back sharply defined.

Lining of the mouth is dark with no lighter area on the gums next to the teeth (as with coho salmon).

Chinook Salmon
SCIENTIFIC NAME
Oncorhynchus tshawytscha
OTHER COMMON NAMES
king salmon, spring salmon
RANGE & HABITAT
ocean waters, major rivers, streams
LENGTH & WEIGHT
To 4+ ft. and 126+ lbs.
LIFESPAN
To 6 years
DIET & SUGGESTED BAIT/LURES
Eats sardines, herring, anchovy, squid, Dungeness crab larvae, and krill. Try trolling with bait fish (above), spoons, flashers with hoochies, or mooching; casting wet flies, spoons, and spinners.

Freshwater: Silvery color becomes darker; females become nearly black. Larger males often have blotchy, dull red sides; smaller males turn dull yellow.

Life History & Other Notes

Chinook salmon are members of the salmon family, whose major characteristic is their ability to jump out of the water. This ability allows them to jump over barriers that might otherwise prevent their movement up rivers or streams. The ability to jump over barriers gives Chinook salmon a distinct advantage over other species of fish for growth and survival.

Chinook salmon are very strongly anadromous. Self-maintaining landlocked populations are rare; they sometimes survive in lakes and reservoirs but usually fail to reproduce successfully. Landlocked Chinook salmon are generally much smaller than their anadromous counterparts.

Most anadromous Chinook salmon migrate to fresh water in the fall; the exact time varies from river to river. Fall-run salmon normally enter a stream late enough so that a suitable supply of cool water is available for spawning. Spawning usually occurs between October and January.

Some Chinook salmon enter rivers in the spring. These salmon move upstream until they find a cool area, where they remain throughout the summer to spawn in the fall. Spring runs usually coincide with snow melt and spring runoff, which provide an ample supply of cold water that allows the salmon to reach the upper parts of a stream.

Chinook salmon spawn in cool to cold water streams with gravel bottoms. Females dig nests in the gravel where they deposit a portion of their eggs. Waiting males immediately fertilize the eggs, which are then covered with gravel by the action of females digging another nest directly upstream. The adult salmon may live for up to two weeks after spawning, but all die afterwards.

The eggs hatch in 50 to 60 days. Most young fish migrate to the ocean during their first few months of life, returning to the stream of their birth to spawn when mature, at 3 to 6 years of age.

Sportfishing for salmon in the ocean is done primarily by trolling. Bait including sardines, herring, anchovy or squid can be used. Lures such as spoons or flashers with hoochies can also be used. Salmon fishing occurs from private boats and partyboats, with the largest part of the salmon partyboat fleet fishing from San Francisco Bay ports. These boats are operated by knowledgeable men and women who show their passengers how to catch salmon.

When salmon are biting well in the rivers they are pursued by anglers fishing from shore and boat. Wet flies, spoons and spinners are often successfully used by anglers when fishing for salmon in rivers.

White Sturgeon

J. Tomelleri

— to 12+ ft. —

White sturgeon are native to California. At sea, white sturgeon are found all along the coast, but they are rare south of Monterey. They are most abundant in the Sacramento-San Joaquin river system, particularly in San Pablo Bay. They have also been found in the Russian and Klamath rivers.

Distinguishing Characteristics
Grayish white. Body long and roughly cylindrical. Upper lobe of the tail much larger than lower lobe. Snout broad and short. Mouth toothless and sucker-like, located beneath the head and a short distance behind the eyes. Four barbels on underside of snout, nearer the tip than the mouth. Skin smooth, but with longitudinal rows of heavy bony plates (38 to 48), each with a sharp spine. In very old fish, the spines may be worn away.

Life History & Other Notes
Sturgeon feed by cruising close to the bottom. The barbels ahead of the mouth are sensitive to odor and taste, so that when something edible is detected the mouth drops down and the food is sucked in. Young sturgeon eat mostly small crustaceans; larger sturgeon also feed on clams, fish, and fish egg including winter herring spawn i San Francisco Bay.

CDFW studies indicate tha in late winter and spring adul sturgeon migrate upstream into th Delta, using both the Sacrament and San Joaquin river channels Some travel well up the Sacrament River past the mouth of the Feathe River. By summer most adults hav returned to the bays.

In the Sacramento River, spawn ing occurs between mid-Februar

White Sturgeon
SCIENTIFIC NAME
Acipenser transmontanus
RANGE & HABITAT
Ocean and bay waters, Delta and major rivers
LENGTH & WEIGHT
To 12+ ft. and 1,387 lb.

DIET / SUGGESTED BAIT
Feeds on crustaceans, especially grass shrimp and ghost shrimp, as well as fish and fish eggs, especially herring spawn in San Francisco Bay. Try using shrimps, herring (whole and fillets), and herring spawn for bait.

and late May when water temperatures reach 46° to 72° F. Females may spawn half a million eggs or more onto deep gravel riffles or in rocky holes. The fertilized eggs stick to the bottom and hatch after four to 12 days. The young fish stay close to the bottom, and use both rivers and estuaries as nursery areas. The locations of sturgeon nursery areas are determined at least partly by river flow; more young fish are washed into the estuary when freshwater flows are high. Young sturgeon become increasingly tolerant of salt water as they develop.

Smaller fish (under 40 in.) are present in the Delta year-round. While at sea, some white sturgeon travel long distances. Fish tagged in the San Francisco Bay estuary have been recaptured as far away as Oregon and Washington. Sturgeon have also been caught as far south as Ensenada, Baja California.

The sturgeon family includes some of the largest fishes found in fresh water; some are among the largest fishes in the world. In California, there are confirmed reports of specimens up to 12½ feet in length, and weighing up to 1,387 lbs. The largest sturgeon were caught before 1900 when size records were vague. However, the largest of these fish was probably more than 13 ft. long, weighed more than 1,300 lb, and was likely close to 100 years old. The largest white sturgeon captured in California waters during the past 40 years was a 468 lb. fish caught by a sport angler in the Carquinez Strait in 1983. This fish is the world record sport-caught white sturgeon, as of the printing of this book.

In a University of California, Davis study of white sturgeon in San Francisco Bay during the 1980s, sturgeon were caught, measured, examined for sex and stage of maturity, and released. Median male size was 3.6 ft. and median female size was 4.6 ft.

The recreational fishery for sturgeon encompasses a very large area from San Francisco Bay through the Delta, the Feather River, and the Sacramento River upstream to Colusa. A small subpopulation of white sturgeon also exists in the Klamath River. Grass shrimp, ghost shrimp, herring (whole and fillets) and herring spawn make excellent bait for white sturgeon.

*S*port anglers come from all over the world to fish off California's coast, because nowhere else will you find such a variety of ocean gamefish or diversity of saltwater angling adventures. From salmon and Pacific halibut in the northern and central portions of the state, to the warmer water species such as yellowtail, dorado and marlin found down south, to species available nearly statewide like rockfish and albacore, California is an unbeatable playground for saltwater anglers.

Picture yourself slowly breathing in the fresh, salt air. Your boat slowly pushes through the thinning early morning fog covering the ocean off of northern California. You and your buddies hold your cups of coffee in both hands, grateful for the warmth on cold fingers. The fishing rods in their holders are deeply arched due to the 4-pound cannonball weights that keep your bait at the right depth as you troll. Suddenly, one rod tip bounces. You grab the rod and set the hook – the fight is on! Some time later, a chrome-bright Chinook salmon lies on deck. Even though you're sitting down, you still tremble from the adrenaline rush of the experience.

Placing your feet carefully, you scramble over the rocks, avoiding the slippery patches of green algae. Reaching your favorite spot on the rocky central California coast, you bait your hook with a nice sardine that you caught from the pier the day before. You cast out just beyond the surge that breaks on those rocks,

and wait patiently. You are here at the right time–your consultation of tide tables and swell predictions will undoubtedly pay off. Suddenly, you are startled out of your reverie by a vicious strike that nearly takes the rod from your hands. After a dogged battle in which you almost lose the fish in the rocks twice, you land your quarry – a monster that seems to be all head and teeth – a lingcod. You smile as you realize that your family will eat well tonight.

The morning you've been waiting for has finally arrived – your daughter's first sportfishing trip. It turns out to be a good day's fishing – not great, but good. The skipper decides to make one last stop before heading back to the dock. As the deckhand drops the anchor, you cast a plastic swimbait towards the edge of a nearby kelp bed. Wham! Something slams your lure. Your daughter cheers you on in the tug-of-war that ensues. Soon, you are lipping the biggest kelp bass you have ever caught, every inch of two feet. You take this opportunity to teach your daughter the importance of conservation and resource stewardship, explaining to her the importance of this big female to the population as you release it alive and healthy. You'll always remember the expression of pride on her face every time she looked up at you for the rest of the day.

71

Blue Shark

———— to 12+ ft. ————

The blue shark is found statewide. It is common off Southern California for most of the year, but during warm water periods it may move much farther north. Usually it is observed at the surface of the water some distance from shore, where it swims slowly along with the tips of the first dorsal and caudal fins showing.

Distinguishing Characteristics

Blue or light bluish-gray above, and white below. Body elongate and slender; head slender with a long, pointed snout. Up to three rows of functional teeth in each jaw, with 14 or 15 serrated teeth in each side of each jaw. The pectoral fins are long and sickle-shaped.

Life History & Other Notes

Blue sharks do not mature until they attain a length of 7 to 8 feet. Females may produce up to 135 young, but most litters average 20 to 40 young. Like other female sharks, blue sharks give birth to live young.

Once located, blue sharks are easily taken by anglers. Casting bait at a fish or chumming in an area known to be inhabited by blue sharks will usually produce results. Blue sharks tend to "roll up" on the line, so it is necessary to use a long wire leader to avoid cutting the line on the shark's skin.

While not considered a man-eater, they may attack when they sense blood and so should be considered dangerous. Once landed, they should be bled while still alive, and once dead they should be cleaned, skinned, and the meat soaked in lemon juice or vinegar as soon as possible to avoid the taste of urea in the meat.

Blue Shark

SCIENTIFIC NAME
Prionace glauca

OTHER COMMON NAMES
blue whaler, great blue shark

RANGE & HABITAT
Statewide; more common in Southern California waters

LENGTH & WEIGHT
To 12+ ft. and 450 lb.

LIFESPAN
To 20 YEARS

DIET & SUGGESTED BAIT
Mainly eats fishes, squid, and pelagic red crabs. Try dead fish or squid bait; chum with ground anchovies

---

Sevengill Shark

———— to 10 ft. ————

The sevengill shark is a fairly common coastal species that is frequently found in bays. They are rarely found at depths greater than 330 ft., but has occasionally been found at depths of over 660 ft. The sevengill shark seems to be most abundant where water temperatures lie between 54° F and 64° F. It tends to prefer rocky reef habitat where kelp beds thrive, although it may also be caught over sand and mud bottoms. The greatest concentration of sevengill sharks off California appears to be in San Francisco and Humboldt bays, both of which serve as nursery grounds for newborn and juvenile sharks. It is also common in Tomales and Monterey bays. On the rare occasion when sevengill sharks are seen off Southern California, they are usually in relatively deep water.

Distinguishing Characteristics
Sandy gray to blackish, spotted sparsely with black. Seven gill slits; one dorsal fin; teeth in upper jaw pointed; teeth in bottom jaw more serrated.

Life History & Other Notes
Female sevengill sharks mature at 7¼ to 8¼ ft., and may bear from 80 to 100 young per pregnancy. This shark is an active predator that feeds at or near the top of the food chain. They may hunt alone, using stealth to ambush smaller prey, or in packs, hunting cooperatively to subdue larger fishes or marine mammals. This is a pugnacious shark that will attempt to bite if given the opportunity.

Sevengill Shark
SCIENTIFIC NAME
Notorhynchus cepedianus
RANGE & HABITAT
Statewide; more common in northern California waters
LENGTH & WEIGHT
To 10 ft. (males to 8+ ft.) and 230+ pounds.
LIFESPAN
To 49 years
DIET & SUGGESTED BAIT
Mainly eats fishes, marine mammals. Use live finfish for bait.

73

Brown Smoothhound Shark

———— to 3 ft. ————

Off California, the brown smoothhound shark is commonly found from Humboldt Bay southward. It is often caught in bays from San Francisco to Point Conception, and prefers sandy, shallow environments, ranging from near shore to 360 ft. depths.

Distinguishing Characteristics

Reddish-brown or bronze above, sides sometimes silvery with white belly. Body elongate, tapering from behind the dorsal fin to the long slender tail. No scales on the latter one-fifth of the dorsal fins; edges of the fins are frayed. Snout comparatively long and flattened. Teeth small, pavement-like, but with sharp points.

Life History & Other Notes

The brown smoothhound shark is a relatively small shark. It is one of the most abundant sharks in the central California sport fishery. The brown smoothhound belongs to the same family of sharks as the gray smoothhound and leopard shark. The gray smoothhound shark (*Mustelus californicus*) is very similar in appearance to this species, but may be differentiated by its blunt teeth and lack of a frayed edge on the dorsal fins. Females bear their young live, as do most other sharks.

The brown smoothhound shark feeds on crabs, shrimp, and small fishes, all of which make good bait. This is a fun sport species to catch on light tackle, and is considered a very good eating fish.

Brown Smoothhound Shark

SCIENTIFIC NAME
Mustelus henlei

OTHER COMMON NAMES
mud shark, dogfish, sand shark

RANGE & HABITAT
From Humboldt Bay south in shallow, sandy environments

LENGTH
To about 3 ft.

LIFESPAN
To 13 years

DIET & SUGGESTED BAIT
Feeds on crab, shrimp, small fishes. Try these items or cut squid as bait

74

to 7 ft.

The beautifully spotted and barred leopard shark is abundant in central and Southern California bays and along sandy beaches, and is also found in northern California bays. It is most common in shallow water to a depth of 15 ft., less so down to 300 ft. or deeper in ocean waters. During the fall, large numbers may be found in San Francisco and Monterey bays.

Distinguishing Characteristics

Easily identified by the gray coloration over most of its body, and the black spots and crossbars on the back and side. Body elongate, with short and bluntly rounded snout. White or pale underneath.

Life History & Other Notes

Leopard sharks eat a variety of fishes and shellfish, including squid, anchovy, and crab. It favors muddy bays and sloughs, especially in northern California, and is known to move in and out with the tides to feed over shallow tidal mudflats. It also occurs along the open coast and around Southern California offshore islands, where it frequents kelp beds, sandy bottoms near rocky reefs, and the surf zone along sandy beaches. As with most sharks, female leopard sharks bear live young.

While this shark is considered relatively harmless and is usually timid around divers, it should be handled with care. Most anglers use rod and reel tackle to take leopard shark; however, some spearfishing for this species does occur. The leopard shark is very good eating, and has been favorably compared to salmon.

Leopard Shark

SCIENTIFIC NAME
Triakis semifasciata

OTHER COMMON NAMES
cat shark

RANGE & HABITAT
Statewide in bay environments, and in shallow waters near sandy beaches and kelp beds in Southern California

LENGTH & WEIGHT
To 7 ft. and 70 lbs.

LIFESPAN
To 30 years

DIET & SUGGESTED BAIT
Feeds on crab, shrimp, mollusks and small fishes. Try these items or cut squid as bait

75

Shortfin Mako Shark

—— to 8 ft. ——

The shortfin mako

shark is usually found off the southern part of the state; it is seldom caught north of Cape Mendocino. This shark travels the oceans worldwide, occurring from the surface to depths of at least 500 ft. It is rarely found in waters where the temperature falls below 60° F.

Distinguishing Characteristics

Dark blue above becoming white on the sides and belly. Long, pointed snout, crescent-shaped tail fin. Keel on each side of the root of the tail; teeth long, sharp, with knife-like edges and without small points at their bases; first dorsal fin inserted behind pectoral base.

Life History & Other Notes

The shortfin mako shark is a top carnivore in the ocean food chain. It is known to prey upon many species of fish including mackerel, sardine, swordfish, tuna, and other sharks, and also squid. In addition, the adult diet may include several species of marine mammals. Like many of its ocean relatives, the shortfin mako shark may eat whatever is abundant in its surroundings.

Like other female sharks, shortfin mako sharks give birth to live young. They are believed to produce from four to 30 young per pregnancy. The Southern California Bight is an important nursery area for young shortfin mako sharks.

The shortfin mako shark should be considered dangerous and handled with all caution. They are a fine game fish, famed for their fight and spectacular leaps. They are often taken by trolling, or by casting live bait to sharks at or near the surface.

Shortfin Mako Shark

SCIENTIFIC NAME
Isurus oxyrinchus
OTHER COMMON NAMES
mackerel shark, bonito shark
RANGE & HABITAT
*Cape Mendocino south,
most common off S. California*
LENGTH & WEIGHT
To 8 ft. and 1,059 lb.
LIFESPAN
To 25 years
DIET & SUGGESTED BAIT
*Eats mostly fishes and squid.
Use live mackerel
or bonito as bait*

Shovelnose Guitarfish

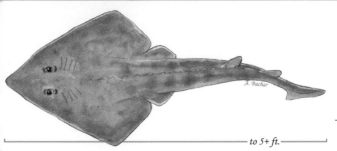

A. Bachar

— to 5+ ft. —

The shovelnose

guitarfish gets its name from its similarity to the musical instrument: head tapered and somewhat round, flattened, and broader than its sturdy, shark-like tail. Off California, shovelnose guitarfish are found from San Francisco Bay southward. It is often caught over sand or mud-sand bottoms in shallow coastal waters to depths of 50 ft.

Shovelnose Guitarfish

SCIENTIFIC NAME
Rhinobatos productus
OTHER COMMON NAMES
shovelnose shark, sand shark
RANGE & HABITAT
San Francisco Bay south in shallow sand or mud environments
LENGTH & WEIGHT
To 5+ ft. and 40 lbs.
LIFESPAN
To 16 years
DIET & SUGGESTED BAIT/LURES
Eats a variety of crustaceans, worms, and clams. Try clams, mussels, or sand crabs as bait, or almost any kind of lure.

Distinguishing Characteristics

Brownish-gray above, lighter below. Body flattened, gradually tapering to the tail; the body disk is longer than it is wide. Snout long, pointed, and rounded at the tip. No dark crossbars on the back; possesses a tail fin and two dorsal fins.

Life History & Other Notes

The shovelnose guitarfish's diet consists of a variety of crustaceans, worms, and clams. It has been observed feeding on sand crabs in water less than 3 in. deep. At times it is left stranded on the beach by receding waves and must wiggle its way back into the water, much like the California grunion.

Shovelnose guitarfish bear live young, as many as 28 pups from one female. Mating takes place during the summer months and the young, born during the following spring and summer, look like 6 in. replicas of the adults.

Shovelnose guitarfish are caught in the surf, in bays, and from piers. It takes live or dead bait including clams, mussels, sand crabs and almost any other bait. Its flesh, especially the tail and back straps, is considered quite tasty.

77

Soupfin Shark

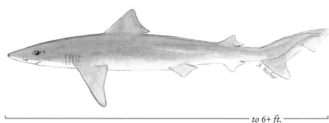

to 6+ ft.

Along the California

coast, the soupfin shark generally may be found from close inshore (including shallow bays, usually near the bottom) to offshore waters at depths of up to 1,500 ft. Males dominate off northern California, while females are primarily found in the south; mid-state, where nursery areas exist in San Francisco and Tomales bays, the ratio of males to females is about equal.

Distinguishing Characteristics

Dark gray or blue-gray above, white below, black on forward edges of dorsal and pectoral fins. Anal fin present; first dorsal fin in front of pelvic fins; no keel on the root of the tail; second dorsal fin directly above and about the same size as anal fin. Prominent spiracle behind the eye.

Life History & Other Notes

Soupfin sharks are highly migratory, moving north during the summer and south or into deeper waters during the winter. They are swift-moving, and can travel up to 35 miles per day. Soupfin sharks are livebearers, with litters averaging 35 pups. The period of gestation is believed to be about one year.

Soupfin sharks eat mostly medium- to small-sized fishes, including bottom dwellers such as flatfishes and rockfishes, and open-water fishes such as mackerel and barracuda.

Soupfin shark liver is the richest known source of vitamin A. During World War II commercial harvest of this species and the spiny dogfish were the chief factors in the production of vitamin A for the United States and the allied nations. Soupfin shark meat is highly prized by recreational anglers.

Soupfin Shark

SCIENTIFIC NAME
Galeorhinus galeus

OTHER COMMON NAMES
tope shark

RANGE & HABITAT
Statewide, nearshore to 1,500 ft.

LENGTH & WEIGHT
To 6+ ft. and 100 lb.

LIFESPAN
To 55 years

DIET & SUGGESTED BAIT
*Eats mostly fishes
and a few invertebrates
such as crab, shrimp and lobster.
Try using live squid for bait
with a wire leader*

Spiny Dogfish

— to 5+ ft. —

Spiny dogfish are common in nearshore waters and along the continental shelf off the California coast. They are generally found to depths of 1,200 ft., although spiny dogfish have been taken at depths of 2,400 ft. They range into deeper waters off southern California, and are often found in schools.

Distinguishing Characteristics

Slate gray to brownish above, sometimes with white spots, becoming white below. Body elongate and slender, head pointed. This species and the horn shark are the only sharks along the California coast with spines at the beginning of both dorsal fins. The mildly poisonous spines are used for defense.

Life History & Other Notes

The spiny dogfish feeds upon practically all smaller fishes such as herring, sardines, anchovies, smelts and even small spiny dogfish. It will also eat crabs.

Most adult spiny dogfish measure from 2 to 4 ft. long. Females are larger than males, and produce from three to 14 young at a time after a gestation period of nearly two years (the longest gestation period of any vertebrate animal). Spiny dogfish are long-lived; as a result, heavy fishing could reduce the population of this slow-growing, low-reproductive species quite rapidly.

Spiny dogfish liver is very rich in vitamin A. During World War II, commercial harvest of this species and soupfin shark were the chief factors in the production of vitamin A for the United States and the allied nations.

Spiny Dogfish

SCIENTIFIC NAME
Squalus acanthias

OTHER COMMON NAMES
dog shark, grayfish, pinback shark, green-eyed grinner

RANGE & HABITAT
Statewide to depths of 2,400 ft.

LENGTH & WEIGHT
To 5+ ft. and 15 lbs.

LIFESPAN
To 75 years

DIET & SUGGESTED BAIT
Eats smaller fishes, crabs. Try fishing with feathered jigs baited with anchovies, crabs, squid, ghost shrimp or small live fish

79

Swell Shark

to 3+ ft.

The swell shark is commonly found near shore off Southern California, particularly around kelp beds; it is uncommon north of Pt. Conception.

Distinguishing Characteristics

Shades of brown tinged with yellowish; barred and spotted with black on back and sides; sides with small whitish spots. Anal fin present; no keels on root of tail base; first dorsal fin far back, above pelvic fins; head broad, blunt and flat; skin thick, scales large and rough; able to inflate belly.

Life History & Other Notes

Swell sharks feed at night on fishes, alive and dead, and on crustaceans. This shark has been observed sucking in prey like a vacuum, while at other times it may rest open-mouthed on the bottom while fish swim in or are swept in by water currents. Swell sharks are sometimes accidentally caught in lobster traps.

This shark fills its belly with air when taken from the water and can distend itself to grotesque proportions, hence its name "swell shark." When submerged, it can inflate its stomach with water if it is threatened, bending its body into a sharp U-shape and grasping its tail fin in its mouth. This defensive behavior can make it difficult for a predator to bite the shark or drag it from a rocky crevice.

Swell sharks are caught by anglers and sport divers, but are not considered a very good eating fish.

Swell Shark

SCIENTIFIC NAME
Cephaloscyllium ventriosum
OTHER COMMON NAMES
puffer shark
RANGE & HABITAT
*Monterey Bay south,
in rocky kelp bed habitat*
LENGTH
To 3+ ft.
DIET & SUGGESTED BAIT
*Eats fishes and
crustaceans.
Use medium tackle and
small fish,
shrimp or crab
for bait*

to 20 ft.

The thresher shark

is found most frequently off the central and southern parts of the state, inhabiting the upper layers of deep offshore waters near the edge of the continental shelf. This shark travels the oceans worldwide, occurring from the surface to depths of at least 200 ft.

Distinguishing Characteristics

Color varies from brownish-gray, bluish or blackish above to silvery, bluish, or golden below. Body moderately elongate, snout short, mouth crescent-shaped. Dorsal, pectoral and ventral fins are blackish; sometimes pectoral and ventral fins have a white dot in the lip. Possesses 21 to 22 teeth on each side of the upper jaw.

Life History & Other Notes

Off California, thresher sharks feed mostly on sardines, anchovies, mackerel and squid. These sharks may use their long tails, which often measure half of their total length, as a flail to frighten or stun prey.

Thresher sharks caught off California are often taken on live sardines, anchovies, or mackerel, or on trolled lures. The best fishing areas include the inshore coastal water between Point Conception and Port Hueneme, and Santa Monica Bay, especially around Malibu and Paradise Cove.

Thresher sharks are most abundant in the summer months. Considered a fine game fish on light or medium tackle, they can put on quite an aerial display, leaping completely out of the water. They are highly esteemed as a good-eating fish.

Thresher Shark

SCIENTIFIC NAME
Alopias vulpinus

OTHER COMMON NAMES
common thresher, longtail shark

RANGE & HABITAT
*Statewide, mostly from
Point Conception south*

LENGTH & WEIGHT
To 20 ft. and 1,000 lbs.

LIFESPAN
To 19 years

DIET & SUGGESTED BAIT
*Eats mostly sardines, anchovies,
mackerel and squid. Try using a live
mackerel on a 9/0 hook attached to
10 ft. of heavy wire leader*

81

Bat Ray

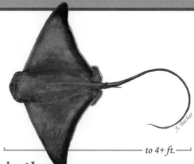

to 4+ ft.

The bat ray is the

only member of the eagle ray family to inhabit California's coastal waters. It is found statewide along the open coast on flat rocky bottoms, in sand patches among rocks, and in kelp beds, but is more common in bays and sloughs. Adults tend to congregate in groups, and are often found resting on the bottom. Even so, solitary individuals are not uncommon.

Distinguishing Characteristics

Dark brown to dark olive or almost black above, white below. Distinct head elevated above the body disk. Tail whip-like and as long or longer than the width of the body disk; sting located just behind body. No arm-like projections on head.

Life History & Other Notes

Bat rays feed chiefly upon mollusks and crustaceans. In bays and sloughs prey includes clams, oysters, shrimp and crabs. On the open coast they eat abalone, various other marine snails, and mollusks. To find clams, bat rays swim along the bottom until they encounter a current of water expelled by the clam. The ray then exposes the clams by flapping its wings.

Mating takes place during the summer months, and the young are born alive after a one-year gestation period. The young are always born tail-first with their wings rolled up over their bodies.

Most sportfishing for bat rays takes place in protected bays and estuaries. Although bat rays may be taken in the open ocean, anglers prefer to catch them in sheltered waters. Heavy tackle is recommended since anglers may encounter large rays.

Bat Ray

SCIENTIFIC NAME
Myliobatis californica

OTHER COMMON NAMES
sting ray, mud marlin

RANGE & HABITAT
Statewide, often in bays and sloughs

LENGTH & WEIGHT
To 4+ ft. and 181 lb.

DIET & SUGGESTED BAIT
Feeds on clams, oysters, shrimp, crab, abalone & other snails. Try shrimp, squid, clam, crab, or cut mackerel for bait

---

82

Round Stingray

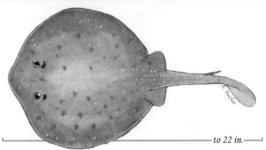

to 22 in.

Round stingray may

be found from Humboldt Bay southward off California, but are more common south of Point Conception. They live on sand or muddy bottoms along beaches and in bays and sloughs. Round stingrays are most often found in water ranging from a few inches to at least 70 ft. deep, but they are most common in about 15 ft. of water.

Distinguishing Characteristics

Brown, often mottled or spotted; underside white to orange. Body disk nearly circular. The round stingray is the only ray in California with both a stinger (located on the tail) and a true tail fin. Other rays have either a whip-like tail or a very short tail with no fin membrane.

Life History & Other Notes

Round stingrays obtain much of their food by burrowing into the sea floor. Their diet includes worms, crabs, snails, clams, and small fishes.

Mating occurs from May to June, and in December. Gestation lasts for about three months, and females give birth to live young, usually from one to six pups per litter.

Native Americans made use of round stingray stingers as spear tips. This stingray is potentially dangerous because of the wound it can inflict. If an angler is stung, the wound should be cleaned thoroughly and bathed in water, and proper medical attention should be sought.

Round stingrays will take almost any of the baits used in surf and bay fishing, but seem particularly fond of marine worms and pieces of clam.

Round Stingray

SCIENTIFIC NAME
Urobatis halleri

OTHER COMMON NAMES
stingray, stingeree

RANGE & HABITAT
*Humboldt Bay south,
most common south of
Pt. Conception*

LENGTH & WEIGHT
To 22 in. and ~2 lb.

DIET & SUGGESTED BAIT
*Feeds on worms, crabs, snails,
clams, and small fishes.
Try worms, squid, or
pieces of clam
for bait*

83

Thornback

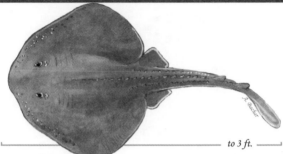

to 3 ft.

T h o r n b a c k s   a r e rays, and are often found in shallow, nearshore waters resting on sandy bottoms partially or completely buried in the sediments. They are common off Southern California, but are a rare find north of Monterey Bay.

Thornbacks are usually found in water less than 18 ft. deep, but have been recorded at depths of over 400 ft. They are primarily found on the mud and sand bottoms of bays and sloughs, lagoons, coastal beaches, and in and around kelp forests. Thornbacks are known to concentrate in large numbers in certain coastal bays and sloughs, including Elkhorn Slough in Central California.

Distinguishing Characteristics
Brown or brownish olive above; belly white or buff. Three rows of strong spines along middle of back and tail; patches of spines on shoulders and near eyes. Body disk wider than it is long. Two dorsal fins (first dorsal fin at mid-tail) and tail fin present; snout broadly rounded. Skin fairly smooth, covered with fine shagreen.

Life History & Other Notes
Thornbacks are livebearers. Mating occurs in the summer with birthing the following summer (usually in August). Litter sizes range from one to 15 pups.

The thornback's prey includes marine worms, crabs, shrimp, squid, and small fishes such as anchovies, gobies, sardines, sculpins, and surfperches. They are fairly docile rays, and are easily approached by divers.

Thornback
SCIENTIFIC NAME
Platyrhynoides triseriata
OTHER COMMON NAMES
*California thornback,
prickleback shark*
RANGE & HABITAT
*Monterey Bay south in sandy and
muddy nearshore environments,
especially bays
and sloughs*
LENGTH
To 3 ft.
DIET & SUGGESTED BAIT
*Eats worms, crabs, shrimp, squid,
and small fishes. Squid and
anchovies work best for bait*

California Grunion

———— to 7+ in. ————

The California

grunion is usually found south of Morro Bay, but they have been taken on occasion as far north as San Francisco Bay. Most often they school a short distance from shore in 15 to 40 ft. of water.

Distinguishing Characteristics

Bluish-green above, silvery below. Bright silvery-blue band, bordered with violet on the upper margin, runs the length of the body. Body elongate; mouth small. Scales small, smooth, and firm. Two dorsal fins, the first with spines; no adipose fin.

Life History & Other Notes

The spawning behavior of the California grunion is one of the most unusual of all marine fishes. They are the only California fish known to strand themselves on the beach to deposit their reproductive products in the moist sand. Females, accompanied by up to eight males, swim with waves washing onto the beach, dig into the sand up to the pectoral fins, and lay eggs. The males wrap themselves around the female and fertilize the eggs. With the next wave, the fish return to the sea. Spawning takes place from early March through September, and then only for three or four nights following the full moon immediately after high tide. Most females spawn from four to eight times per year, and may produce up to 3,000 eggs every two weeks.

CDFW publishes a schedule of predicted grunion runs on its website (below). Observing a grunion run is fascinating, and the fish are also good eating.

www.dfg.ca.gov/marine/grunion.asp

California Grunion

SCIENTIFIC NAME
Leuresthes tenuis

OTHER COMMON NAMES
little smelt, lease smelt

RANGE & HABITAT
Morro Bay south in surf environments

LENGTH & WEIGHT
To 7+ in. and less than 2 oz.

LIFESPAN
To 4 years

DIET/FISHING INFORMATION
Feeds on small crustaceans and fish eggs. Generally caught during spawning runs – may only be taken by hand

---

Silversides

topsmelt — to 14+ in.

jacksmelt — to 22 in.

J a c k s m e l t   a n d topsmelt are members of the silversides family. They are among the most common fishes taken by pier anglers, and are also caught in the surf. Silversides may be caught statewide, and are common in bays, sloughs, and other inshore areas. Within San Francisco Bay, topsmelt are particularly abundant in the shallow subtidal and intertidal waters of the South Bay.

Distinguishing Characteristics

Jacksmelt and topsmelt may look very much the same to the casual observer. Any silversides over 14½ in. may be assumed to be jacksmelt. The two species may be differentiated by noting the location of the first dorsal fin: For jacksmelt, the first dorsal fin is placed ahead of the vent (anus); for topsmelt the first dorsal fin is just about directly over the vent. Both are silvery, elongate fish with a midline stripe; jacksmelt tend to be greenish-blue above while topsmelt are bright green above.

Life History & Other Notes

Topsmelt feed on plankton and crustaceans; intertidal inhabitants also feed on fly larvae and algae.

They spawn from April through October, attaching egg masses to eelgrass, low-growing algae, and possibly kelp in harbors and bays.

Jacksmelt spawn from October through March, attaching large masses of eggs to shallow water seaweeds. They feed on small crustaceans and fishes. Larger jacksmelt will take a small spinner or artificial flies. Try using small hooks baited with squid, suspended beneath a bobber. Silversides are excellent fighters.

Silversides

SCIENTIFIC NAME
Atherinopsis californiensis
Atherinops affinis

OTHER COMMON NAMES
jacksmelt; topsmelt

RANGE & HABITAT
Statewide in bays, sloughs & surf

LENGTH
Jacksmelt to 22 in.
Topsmelt to 14+ in.

LIFESPAN
Jacksmelt to 11 years
Topsmelt to 9 years

DIET & SUGGESTED BAIT/LURES
Eats small crustaceans, shrimp, snails, and plant matter. Try fishing with artificial flies or shrimp/squid

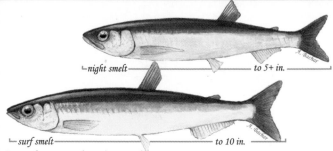

night smelt ┘   to 5+ in.

surf smelt ┘   to 10 in.

Surf smelt (or day

smelt) and night smelt are members of the true smelt family. As their names imply, night smelt spawn at night, and surf (or day) smelt spawn during the day. Both are most common from Monterey Bay northward, and usually congregate near river mouths.

Distinguishing Characteristics

The two species can be differentiated by noting the size of the mouth: In surf smelt, the mouth does not reach past the pupil of the eye; in night smelt the mouth extends at least to the back edge of the pupil. Both have abdominal pelvic fins and an adipose fin. Surf smelt are silver with a purplish hue, back light green. Night smelt are silver, and brownish-green on the back.

Life History & Other Notes

Spawning takes place in the surf with runs occurring from mid-March into the fall months. Night smelt prefer coarser sand than do surf smelt, and their runs are more erratic. Males of both species congregate in dense schools in shallow water, waiting to follow the females as they dash in to deposit their eggs on the sand. Males then fertilize the eggs, and both sexes return to deeper water.

Both species are taken in the surf during spawning runs, using two-man jump nets or one-man A-frame nets that seine the fish from incoming breakers. Some famous smelting beaches include Scott Creek (Santa Cruz County), Portuguese Beach and Russian River (Sonoma County) and Smith River Beach (Del Norte County). Smelt are considered by many to be the best-eating fish in the sea.

Smelt

SCIENTIFIC NAME
Hypomesus pretiosus (surf smelt)
Spirinchus starksi (night smelt)

OTHER COMMON NAMES
day smelt (for surf smelt)

RANGE & HABITAT
North of Long Beach (surf smelt)
North of Pt. Arguello (night smelt)

LENGTH
Surf smelt to 10 in.
Night smelt to 5+ in.

LIFESPAN
Surf smelt to 5 yrs.
Night smelt to 3 yrs.

DIET
Small crustaceans, plankton

Jack Mackerel

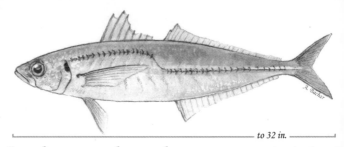

— to 32 in. —

J a c k   m a c k e r e l are found from the surface to a depth of 150 ft. off California, and up to 500 miles offshore. They are an open-ocean, schooling species often found at or near the surface in close proximity to the mainland shore, islands, and offshore banks.

Distinguishing Characteristics

Metallic blue to olive green above, becoming silvery below. Dark spot on edge of gill cover. Body elongate, tapering to a tail that is as broad as it is deep. Enlarged scales along side; last rays of the dorsal and anal fins attached to the body.

Life History & Other Notes

Jack mackerel are known to feed heavily upon anchovies, lanternfish, and juvenile squid, and often take crustaceans and small, free-swimming mollusks as well. Spawning takes place from March through June, and occurs over an extensive area from 80 to over 240 miles offshore.

Jack mackerel can live for 20 to 30 years and attain weights of 4 to 5 lb. Larger fish may be solitary. For fish with such a long life span, they become sexually active at a very young age (2 to 3 years). They are quite common near the islands and banks off Southern California when less than 4 years old, after which they presumably move offshore or northward.

Young jack mackerel do not feed extensively on anchovies or bite readily on baited hooks or lures, thus they are not caught very often by sport anglers. Anglers may successfully jig for them, however, with small feathered hooks. The best fishing months include July, August and September.

Jack Mackerel

SCIENTIFIC NAME
Trachurus symmetricus

OTHER COMMON NAMES
horse mackerel, Spanish mackerel

RANGE & HABITAT
Statewide in upper 150 ft. of water

LENGTH & WEIGHT
To 32 in. and 5 lb.

LIFE SPAN
To 30 years

DIET & SUGGESTED BAIT/LURES
Anchovy, lanternfish, squid, crustaceans, small free-swimming mollusks. Try jigging for young fish using small feathered hooks

Pacific Chub Mackerel

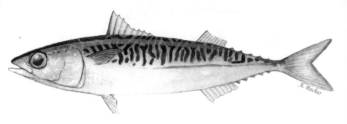

— to 25 in. —

The Pacific chub

mackerel travels temperate seas worldwide to depths of 150 ft. Off California, however, they are seldom caught north of Monterey Bay. They are a schooling species most frequently caught within 20 miles of shore.

Distinguishing Characteristics

Dark blue head and back with about 30 dark, wavy lines. Undersides silver-green. Elongated body tapers at both ends. Widely separated first and second dorsal fins, four to six dorsal finlets behind second dorsal fin.

Life History & Other Notes

Pacific chub mackerel prefer to feed on larval, juvenile, and small adult fishes. They also eat small crustaceans and, to a lesser extent, squid.

Off Southern California, spawning normally reaches it peak during the early spring months, especially March, April and May. The tiny eggs float free in upper ocean waters, usually within 300 ft. of the surface. At average water temperatures, the eggs hatch in four to five days.

Known as a voracious and indiscriminant feeder, Pacific chub mackerel will devour live anchovy, engulf dead cut bait, strike readily on lures and often on flies. When in a feeding frenzy, it has even been known to hit a piece of rag soaked in fish blood. While it is relatively small in size, ounce for ounce it scores high for power and beauty. Pacific chub mackerel put up an excellent fight on light tackle. They make tasty fare when smoked, barbequed or broiled.

Pacific Chub Mackerel

SCIENTIFIC NAME
Scomber japonicus

OTHER COMMON NAMES
American mackerel, blue mackerel, greenback mackerel

RANGE & HABITAT
Statewide in upper 150 ft. of water; most common south of Monterey Bay

LENGTH & WEIGHT
To 25 in. and ~6 lb.

LIFE SPAN
To 12 years

DIET & SUGGESTED BAIT/LURES
Fishes, squid, small crustaceans. Try anchovy or cut squid for bait, also lures or flies

89

Barred Surfperch

to 17 in.

Barred surfperch are found south of Bodega Bay off California. They prefer the surf zone along sandy beaches where they seem to congregate in depressions on the bottom. They have, however, been taken as deep as 240 ft.

Distinguishing Characteristics

Olive green to yellow on the back, becoming silver below; with bronze brassy stripes or yellow vertical bars and spots on the side. Lower jaw slightly shorter than upper; no red or reddish color on the fins. The barred surfperch is one of three marine surfperches living off sandy beaches with similar color and markings. Its shorter lower jaw and lack of red in the fins helps to distinguish it from calico and redtail surfperches.

Life History & Other Notes

Barred surfperch mainly feed on sand crabs, but will also eat bean clams and smaller crustaceans .

This surfperch gives birth to live young from March through July. As few as four to as many as 113 young have been counted per female, but the average is 33 young. The young are about 2½ in. long at birth, and mature at about 6½ in. long, when 1 to 2 years old. Barred surfperch are relatively short-lived. The oldest males reach about 6 years old and 12 in. long, and the oldest females reach about 9 years old and 17 in. long.

The most popular bait for barred surfperch is soft-shelled sand crabs, but blood worms, mussels, cut fish and small lures such as plastic worms or flies also work well. Fishing is usually best on an incoming tide when the perch are feeding inside the breaker zone.

Barred Surfperch
SCIENTIFIC NAME
Amphistichus argenteus
OTHER COMMON NAMES
sand perch
RANGE & HABITAT
Bodega Bay south off sandy beaches
LENGTH & WEIGHT
To 17 in. and 4.5 lb.
LIFE SPAN
To 10+ years
DIET & SUGGESTED BAIT/LURES
Sand crabs, bean clams, small crabs. Try fishing with soft-shelled sand crabs, blood worms, mussels, cut fish, and small lures such as plastic worms and flies

90

Black Perch

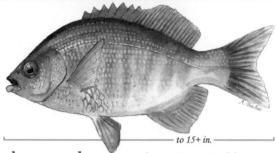

to 15+ in.

Black perch are
found from Fort Bragg southward off California, over seaweed-covered rocky bottoms, around piers and kelp beds along the outer coast, and near eelgrass beds in bays. They are frequently found swimming singly or in groups of three or four among rocks and caves at an average depth of 20 ft., but can be found from the intertidal zone to a depth of 150 ft.

Distinguishing Characteristics
Olive green or reddish brown, about nine vertical bars on sides, thick orange-brown to yellow lips. Dark to light blue bar at the base of the anal fin. In the San Francisco area during fall and winter, some turn jet black with blue crescents in the middle of their scales. This coloring along with a row of small scales along the base of the anal fin rays and a patch of enlarged scales between the pectoral and pelvic fins serve to identify this species.

Life History & Other Notes
In addition to eating a variety of fish, black perch also pick parasites from other fish, as do senoritas and kelp perch.

Breeding takes place mainly during the summer, but possibly occurs throughout the year. Adults congregate in dense schools during the breeding season, then pair off. The young are born live predominantly in the spring and summer.

Black perch are caught year-round from rocky shores and piers, most often in bays. They are most abundant in Southern California, but considerable numbers are taken as far north as Tomales Bay.

Black Perch

SCIENTIFIC NAME
Embiotoca jacksoni

OTHER COMMON NAMES
black surfperch, buttermouth, pogie

RANGE & HABITAT
Fort Bragg south, over rocky kelp beds or bay eelgrass beds

LENGTH & WEIGHT
To 15+ inches and ~2 lb.

DIET & SUGGESTED BAIT
Small invertebrates including crustaceans, mollusks, and marine worms.
Try fishing with shrimp, marine worms, or bits of fish flesh

91

Calico Surfperch

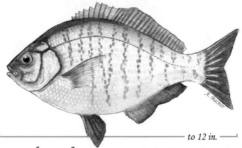

— to 12 in. —

Calico surfperch are

found statewide off sandy beaches, although they can sometimes be found over rocky areas or schooling near pier pilings as well. Calico surfperch are most abundant between San Simeon and Bodega Bay, to a depth of 30 ft.

Distinguishing Characteristics

Silvery with olive green mottling; sides with series of brown speckles that form rough narrow vertical bars; pectoral fins plain, other fins usually reddish except for the caudal fin, which is dark. Lower jaw protrudes beyond upper jaw. Lower edge of eye below upper lip.

Calico surfperch are often mistaken for redtail surfperch. The best way to determine which species you have is to compare the spiny dorsal fins. For calico surfperch, it is about as high as the second, soft dorsal fin, while for redtail surfperch, the angular spiny dorsal fin is much higher than the second, soft dorsal fin.

Life History & Other Notes

As with all surfperches, calico surfperch bear live young. They will produce from three to 10 young per pregnancy, with larger females

producing larger broods of young.

Calico surfperch prefer to eat small crustaceans such as sand crabs and shrimp.

December and January are the best months for surfperch fishing, and calico surfperch fishing is best along Monterey Bay beaches. Calico surfperch (and other surfperches) can be caught from shore using a spinning or casting outfit with 10 to 15 lb. test monofilament line, and a standard two-hook leader with no. 6 hooks.

Calico Surfperch

SCIENTIFIC NAME
Amphistichus koelzi

OTHER COMMON NAMES
porgee

RANGE & HABITAT
Statewide off sandy beaches

LENGTH & WEIGHT
To 12 in. and 2 lb.

DIET & SUGGESTED BAIT/LURES
*Eats sand crabs, shrimp,
and other small crustaceans.
Try fishing with
soft-shelled sand crabs,
blood worms, mussels,
cut fish or small lures*

92

to 17+ in.

Pile perch are found

statewide in a variety of coastal water habitats: in bays and estuaries, near piers and other underwater structures, and off rocky shores and kelp beds, from the surface to a depth of 240 ft. They prefer rugged, rocky habitat and dense algal growth that harbors abundant prey.

Distinguishing Characteristics

Silvery with brown or sooty overtones; most heavily pigmented on dorsal surface. Fins dusky. Rays at front of soft dorsal fin about twice as long as first dorsal fin spines. Usually with a dark vertical bar mid-body. Tail fin deeply forked.

Life History & Other Notes

Pile perch feed on hard-shelled mollusks, crabs, barnacles, and other crustaceans they find along the sea floor. In addition to these food items, pile perch have been observed picking parasites from other fish, as do black perch and senoritas. Adults commonly travel in schools of 50 to 100 fish in cooler, deeper water during the summer and fall; they travel to shallower water during winter and spring. This seasonal movement may be caused by a preference for water temperatures of 61° F or lower.

Mating takes place in the fall, with females giving birth to between 7 and 80 live young. Young pile perch are born in the spring and summer during times of dense kelp growth. The young use the kelp understory as refuge from predators, as do young rubberlip seaperch, striped seaperch, and other young fish.

Pile perch may be taken from piers, jetties, skiffs, and from shore.

Pile Perch

SCIENTIFIC NAME
Rhacochilus vacca

OTHER COMMON NAMES
dusky perch, piler perch

RANGE & HABITAT
Statewide in a broad variety of habitats

LENGTH
To 17+ in.

LIFE SPAN
To 10 years

DIET & SUGGESTED BAIT
Hard-shelled mollusks, crabs, barnacles, other crustaceans. Try using mussels, clams, sand worms, cut shrimp or similar bait.

Rainbow Seaperch

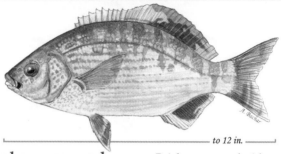

—— to 12 in. ——

Rainbow seaperch are

found from Cape Mendocino south off California, usually near rocky areas, often in and around kelp beds to depths of 130 ft. They are not normally found in or near the surf area.

Distinguishing Characteristics
Red and blue stripes on sides; pelvic fins bright blue and red-orange. Belly long and straight between the pelvic and anal fins; dark blotches on the soft dorsal and anal fins.

Life History & Other Notes
Rainbow seaperch feed on small crustaceans, snails, and marine worms. They have also been observed cleaning parasites from other fish, as do pile perch and kelp perch.

As with all surfperches, rainbow seaperch bear live young, with a brood size of nine to 22 young per pregnancy. Brood size tends to increase with the size of the female, as with all other saltwater perches. Mating season takes place between April and September. After a 5- to 6-month pregnancy, females give birth to live young in coastal embayments including Tomales Bay, Bodega Bay, Monterey Bay, and San Francisco Bay.

Rainbow seaperch (along with most perches) are fairly easy to catch, and are highly sought. They can be caught using light gear and a variety of baits including fresh mussel, pile worms, bloodworms, or small live crabs. A spinning or casting outfit using 10 to 15 lb. test monofilament fishing line, and a standard two-hook leader is ideal for seaperch and other saltwater perches.

Rainbow Seaperch
SCIENTIFIC NAME
Hypsurus caryi
OTHER COMMON NAMES
rainbow surfperch
RANGE & HABITAT
Cape Mendocino south, in and around rocks and kelp beds
LENGTH
To 12 in.
DIET & SUGGESTED BAIT
Eats small crustaceans, snails, marine worms. Try fishing with fresh mussels, pile worms, bloodworms, or small live crabs

94

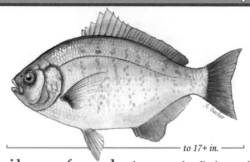

← to 17+ in. →

Redtail surfperch

occur from Monterey Bay north off California. They are the most frequently caught species of surfperch north of Bodega Bay. This species is predominantly a surf-dweller off sandy beaches, but has also been taken in rocky areas adjacent to beaches. They are common in estuaries and protected embayments during spawning season.

Distinguishing Characteristics

Silver with olive green mottling and bars on the side. Tail pink to deep purple. Body oval; upper head is nearly straight from the snout to the dorsal fin, except for a slight depression above the eye.

Life History & Other Notes

Small crabs, shrimp and other crustaceans are the major food items preferred by this species; however, mussels and marine worms are also eaten.

Like all surfperches, the redtail gives birth to live young. Just before spawning in the spring and early summer, redtail surfperch congregate in sheltered inshore waters. Breeding season is in the fall, and the young are born in the following spring and summer, primarily from June to August. Females may give birth to up to 51 young, but average 27 young per pregnancy.

The average size of redtail surfperch landed by sport anglers is 1.5 to 2 lb., although 3 lb. fish are not uncommon. Light tackle using crab backs for bait is preferred in Humboldt Bay, while heavier tackle using sand crabs, tube worms or clams for bait works well when surf fishing.

Redtail Surfperch

SCIENTIFIC NAME
Amphistichus rhodoterus

OTHER COMMON NAMES
porgie, rosy surf fish

RANGE & HABITAT
Monterey Bay north, in surf environments

LENGTH
To 17+ in.

LIFE SPAN
To 9 years

DIET & SUGGESTED BAIT
Small crabs, shrimp, mussels, marine worms. Try fishing with sand crabs, tube worms, or clams

95

Rubberlip Seaperch

to 18+ in.

Rubberlip seaperch are found from Russian Gulch State Beach (Mendocino County) southward off California, from the surface to a depth of 150 ft. They are the largest of the surfperches off our coast, reaching a maximum length of 18½ inches. They prefer rocky areas, kelp beds, and dense algal growth that harbors abundant prey.

Distinguishing Characteristics

Silvery with blue to purple coloration on dorsal surface; pectoral fins yellowish and pelvic fins black; other fins dusky or fringed with black. Thick lips are white or pink.

Life History & Other Notes

Rubberlip seaperch feed at night, mostly eating small, thin-shelled invertebrates including shrimp, small crabs, and mollusks, along with algae. They are picky eaters, mouthing various items of interest and spitting out the items they decide not to eat.

Young rubberlip seaperch are born in the summer months during times of dense kelp growth. They use the kelp understory as cover along with young pile perch, striped seaperch and other young fish.

Rubberlip seaperch are taken from piers, jetties, skiffs, and from shore. Adults will occasionally form mixed schools with pile perch. Rubberlip seaperch are not only the largest, but also reputed to be the tastiest of the surfperches. Try using fresh mussels, live marine worms or small pieces of shrimp for bait. Rubberlip seaperch may also be taken with plastic grubs.

Rubberlip Seaperch

SCIENTIFIC NAME
Rhacochilus toxotes

OTHER COMMON NAMES
rubberlip surfperch, sprat, liver lip

RANGE & HABITAT
Russian Gulch State Beach southward in bays and rocky areas with dense algae growth

LENGTH & WEIGHT
To 18+ in. and 2+ lb.

LIFE SPAN
To 10 years

DIET & SUGGESTED BAIT
Small shrimp, amphipods, crabs, mollusks, occasionally algae. Try shrimp, marine worms, or mussels for bait.

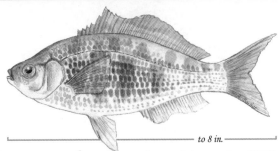

to 8 in.

Shiner perch may

be found statewide in calmer ocean waters. They prefer bays around eelgrass beds, and the pilings of wharfs and piers. Shiner perch have been captured in trawl nets in 350 to 480 ft. of water and have been observed at a depth of 120 ft. by divers, but they are more numerous in shallow areas.

Distinguishing Characteristics

Gray to greenish above with vertical lemon yellow crossbars in the shape of the number "711" with eight horizontal sooty lines along the sides. During courtship and breeding the males are dark gray, almost black in color, and have a black spot on each side of the snout. Much more slender than the similar island surfperch found in the Channel Islands.

Life History & Other Notes

Shiner perch eat mostly small crustaceans and other invertebrates. They are frequently observed around pier pilings nipping the appendages off of barnacles.

Mating takes place during the summer months, and the young are born the following spring and summer. During courtship, the male closely follows the female, their movements remarkably well synchronized.

Shiner perch may be caught from shore, docks, piers, rocks, and almost any other fishing area. They are probably the fish most frequently caught by young anglers. They can be taken on almost any type of bait and any type of fishing equipment, from handlines to spinning gear, so long as the baited hook is small enough to fit in the fish's mouth.

Shiner Perch

SCIENTIFIC NAME
Cymatogaster aggregata

OTHER COMMON NAMES
shiner surfperch, 7-11 perch, yellow shiner

RANGE & HABITAT
Statewide in bays around piers and eelgrass beds

LENGTH & WEIGHT
To 8 in. and ~3 oz.

LIFE SPAN
To ~3 years

DIET & SUGGESTED BAIT
Small crustaceans and invertebrates such as barnacles. Will take just about any bait offered on a small hook

97

Silver Surfperch

to 10+ in.

Silver surfperch are found statewide, primarily in the sandy surf zones, although they are sometimes caught among shallow rocks from piers and in bays as well. They are plentiful, easy to catch, and occur in large numbers in surf, shore, and pier creels. Silver surfperch are found to a depth of 360 ft.

Distinguishing Characteristics

Silvery with dusky (brownish to gray) coloration on the back and dusky bars on the sides. Body oval and flattened (The species name *ellipticum* refers to the silver surfperch's elliptical, or oval, body outline), head small with moderately large mouth. Tail usually pink with an occasional orange spot on the anal fin. No black coloration on the pelvic fins (as with walleye surfperch).

Life History & Other Notes

The silver surfperch's diet includes shrimp and other crustaceans, and algae. As with all surfperches, the young are born alive and are relatively large. Mating occurs during the fall and early winter months. The male approaches the female from below; both swim with vents close for 2 to 3 seconds, then they separate and repeat the process. Three to sixteen young are born the following spring and summer.

Surfperch in general rank among the top ten fish in numbers caught by recreational anglers in central and northern California.

Silver Surfperch

SCIENTIFIC NAME
Hyperprosopon ellipticum
OTHER COMMON NAMES
silver perch
RANGE & HABITAT
Statewide, but most commonly north of Pt. Conception, off sandy beaches and among shallow rocks
LENGTH & WEIGHT
To 10+ in. and ~2 oz.
LIFE SPAN
To 7 years
DIET & SUGGESTED BAIT
Small shrimp and other crustaceans, and algae. Use light line and small hooks baited with shrimp or squid

Spotfin Surfperch

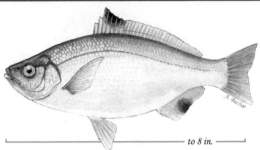

— to 8 in. —

The spotfin surfperch

is most commonly found along sandy beaches in surf zones and out to a depth of 300 ft. They are generally not as common inside of bays as they are in the coastal waters just outside of bays, such as the sandy beaches outside of San Francisco Bay, Monterey Bay and Tomales Bay.

Distinguishing Characteristics

Silver, dusky on back. Large black spots on dorsal and anal fin.

Spotfin Surfperch

SCIENTIFIC NAME
Hyperprosopon anale
RANGE & HABITAT
Statewide off sandy beaches and piers
LENGTH
To 8 in.
LIFE SPAN
To ~4 years
DIET & SUGGESTED BAIT
Squid, marine worms, small crustaceans, jellyfish, algae, fish eggs. Try using light line and small hooks baited with squid

Life History & Other Notes

Spotfin surfperch feed on young squid, marine worms, small crustaceans, algae, jellyfish, and fish eggs.

Like other surfperches, spotfin surfperch are livebearers, and produce from four to 20 young during the summer months. They occupy offshore waters (from 45 to 192 ft. depths) during most of the year, but in the summer months schools composed mostly of females move inshore where the young are born between June and August. When birthing time nears, female spotfin surfperch (and most other female perches) become extremely large and not very agile. In this state, they seek refuge from predators in turbid bay waters, eelgrass beds, and other areas where they and their young can avoid predation. The young also grow more rapidly in warmer, more productive nearshore habitats.

Spotfin surfperch are not commonly landed, but are caught occasionally by pier and surf anglers. They may reach a length of 8 in., but are usually less than 6 in. long.

99

Striped Seaperch

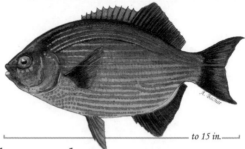

— to 15 in. —

Striped seaperch are

found statewide, but are rarely seen south of Point Conception. They are found to a depth of 55 ft., although they prefer shallow water less than 18 ft. deep. Striped seaperch are often found in rocky areas with dense algal growth including kelp beds, which harbor abundant prey.

Distinguishing Characteristics
Coppery, darker brown dorsally; about 15 horizontal, neon blue stripes on the body below the lateral line; several series of blue spots and stripes on head; fins coppery.

Life History & Other Notes
Striped seaperch have a relatively large mouth which lends itself to a diverse diet, including shrimps, crabs and other crustaceans, marine worms, mollusks, and sometimes brittle stars. They feed throughout the day, selecting prey visually and eating relatively large, heavy prey when it is available.

Young striped seaperch are born in the summer months during times of dense kelp growth, and use the kelp understory as cover along with pile perch, rubberlip seaperch, and other young fish. Although juvenile striped seaperch

and black perch sometimes school together, adults of these species compete for food. Wherever the two species inhabit the same general area, striped seaperch will aggressively eliminate black perch from its immediate home range to a depth of 18 ft.

Striped seaperch are an extremely popular sport fish. They may comprise up to 10 percent of all fishes caught in the recreational fishery (excluding salmon) north of San Francisco.

Striped Seaperch
SCIENTIFIC NAME
Embiotoca lateralis
OTHER COMMON NAMES
striped surfperch, blue perch
RANGE & HABITAT
Statewide, but most common north of Point Conception in rocky areas with dense algae growth
LENGTH & WEIGHT
To 15 in. and 2+ lb.
LIFE SPAN
To 10 years
DIET & SUGGESTED BAIT
Eats shrimp, crabs & other crustaceans, marine worms, mollusks. Use light line and small hooks with a variety of baits.

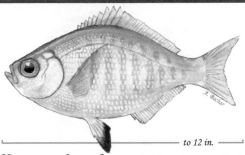

— to 12 in. —

The walleye surfperch

is found in dense schools along sandy beaches, near rocks, and around piers all along the California coast. They may move into embayments such as Humboldt Bay during the summer.

Distinguishing Characteristics

Silver with faint dusky shading on back. Black tips on pelvic fins and black borders on tail and anal fins. Body oval, head small, eyes large. Mouth small and slanted upward.

Walleye Surfperch

SCIENTIFIC NAME
Hyperprosopon argenteum
OTHER COMMON NAMES
China pompano, white perch
RANGE & HABITAT
Statewide off sandy beaches, piers, and near rocks
LENGTH
To 12 in.
LIFE SPAN
To 6 years
DIET & SUGGESTED BAIT
Feeds on small crustaceans. Try shrimp, mussels, pieces of fish, worms, or squid for bait on small hooks

Life History & Other Notes

Walleye surfperch feed mainly on small crustaceans.

Mating takes place from October through December, when dense schools break up and males and females pair off. The encroachment of a single male on a breeding pair is immediately countered by a quick charge from the courting male. Between 5 and twelve young, depending on the size of the female, are born the following spring. Newborn walleye surfperch average a little over 1½ inches long at birth. They reach maturity the following fall and winter; in fact, the largest portion of the breeding population appears to be the young born the previous year.

Walleye surfperch can be caught in the surf, from rocky shores, and from piers anywhere along the open coast. They usually are the most abundant surfperch caught from piers. A small hook baited with mussels, pieces of fish, worms, squid or shrimp will catch walleye surfperch any time of the year. Running across a school of several thousand walleye surfperch can result in a very rewarding fishing experience.

101

Black Croaker

to 15 in.

The black croaker is found along the open coast and in bays and sloughs south of Point Conception, California. They have been observed to a depth of 150 ft., but most are found at around 20 ft. depths. Adults are often found in rocky areas in caves and dark crevices, but they may also be found near sandy areas.

Distinguishing Characteristics

Blackish, with coppery reflections on back, silver below; pelvic fins black. When brought to the surface, may appear bluish or olive. Some have a sand-colored stripe and/or spotting towards the anterior half of the body from the insertion of the second dorsal fin to near the vent; this becomes more distinct at night.

Life History & Other Notes

Black croakers eat small crabs and shrimp, and other small crustaceans. They are most active at night.

Spawning takes place in late spring and early summer. Black croakers emit drumming or croaking noises (hence their name) during the breeding season. Their tiny, colorless eggs drift with the current, hatching within 48 hours. Young black croakers school near rock outcroppings in very shallow water (from 4 to 18 ft.). The young croakers are striped, resembling salema or sargo, and often school with these species. As they become larger, black croakers break away from the school to wander freely among caves and crevices.

As a result of their "retiring ways," black croakers are not commonly caught on rod and reel. They are a good eating fish, however, and a favorite with spear fishermen.

Black Croaker

SCIENTIFIC NAME
Cheilotrema saturnum
OTHER COMMON NAMES
China croaker
RANGE & HABITAT
Point Conception south, in rocky areas or rock/sand interfaces
LENGTH & WEIGHT
To 15 in. and 1.5 lb.
LIFE SPAN
To 20 years
DIET
Small crabs, shrimp, and other crustaceans

California Corbina

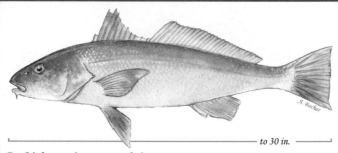

to 30 in.

California corbina

are found from Point Conception southward off California to a depth of 45 ft. Small groups of this species travel along the bottom of sandy beaches and in shallow bays. Adults have been observed feeding in the surf, at times in water so shallow that their backs were exposed.

Distinguishing Characteristics

Uniform gray with incandescent reflections and wavy diagonal lines on sides. Body elongate, head long and mouth small, scarcely reaching a point below the front of the eye. Single barbel on lower jaw. One weak spine at front of anal fin.

Life History & Other Notes

California corbina scoop up mouthfuls of sand, separating the food by sending the sand through their gills. They are very particular feeders, sifting out bits of clam shells and other foreign matter to find sand crab, their preferred prey. They will also eat other crustaceans and clams.

California corbina spawn offshore from June through September, producing free-floating eggs. This species is caught year-round from Southern California's sandy beaches, however fishing is best from July through September. They are very wary and difficult to hook, perhaps because they tend to mouth their food and don't strike solidly very often. Sand crabs are the preferred bait, though anglers can use a variety of invertebrates. An increasing number of anglers pursue corbina with fly fishing tackle. California corbina are very popular sport fish, reserved for sport fishermen only– there is no commercial fishery.

California Corbina

SCIENTIFIC NAME
Menticirrhus undulatus

OTHER COMMON NAMES
king croaker, corbie, bean

RANGE & HABITAT
Pt. Conception south off sandy beaches and in shallow bays

LENGTH & WEIGHT
To 30 in. and 8.5 lb.

LIFE SPAN
To 8+ years

DIET & SUGGESTED BAIT
Eats sand crabs and other crustaceans, clam siphons. Try soft-shelled sand crab, mussel, clam, pile worm, or ghost shrimp for bait on very light line, or flies

103

Spotfin Croaker

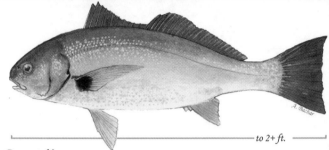

A. Bachar

— to 2+ ft. —

Spotfin croaker are
found most commonly south of
Los Angeles Harbor, but their
official northern range limit is Point
Conception. They live along beaches
and in bays over bottoms that vary
from coarse sand to heavy mud, and
at depths ranging from 4 to 50 ft. or
more. They may prefer depressions
and holes near shore.

Distinguishing Characteristics
Silvery gray with bluish luster above
and white below. Dark wavy lines
on side, large black spot at the base
of the pectoral fin. Body elongate,
but heavy forward. Upper profile
of head steep and slightly curved,
abruptly rounded at the very blunt
snout. Mouth underneath the head.
No barbel. Small spotfin croakers
may be mistaken for small white
croakers, but a count of the dorsal
fins spines will separate the two:
white croakers possess 12 to 15
dorsal fin spines, while the spotfin
has 11 or fewer.

Life History & Other Notes
Spotfin croakers eat a wide variety
of items, but seem to prefer clams,
worms, and small crustaceans. Their
spawning season extends from June
to September.

Spotfin croakers travel considerably from bay to bay, but
without any set pattern. Although
some spotfin croakers are caught
throughout the year, late summer
is best for this species. When a
"croaker hole" is found and a
breeding run is on, good fishing
can be had by all present whether
in a bay, from a pier or in the surf.
This very popular gamefish is
reserved just for sport fishermen-
no commercial fishery exists.

Spotfin Croaker
SCIENTIFIC NAME
Roncador stearnsii
OTHER COMMON NAMES
*Spotties ("golden croakers"
may be male spotfin croakers
in breeding colors)*
RANGE & HABITAT
*Point Conception south, over sand
or mud bottoms*
LENGTH & WEIGHT
To 2+ ft. and 14 lb.
LIFE SPAN
To ~15 years
DIET & SUGGESTED BAIT
*Eats clams, worms, small
crustaceans. Try marine worms,
clams, mussels for bait*

White Croaker

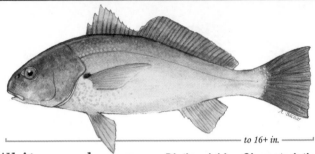

— to 16+ in. —

White croaker may

be found statewide off sandy beaches near and within the surf zone, however it is most abundant from San Francisco Bay southward. They swim in loose schools at or near the bottom, in the surf zone, or in shallow bays and lagoons. Most of the time white croaker are found at depths of 10 to 100 ft. They may on occasion be fairly abundant at depths as great as 600 ft.

White Croaker

SCIENTIFIC NAME
Genyonemus lineatus
OTHER COMMON NAMES
kingfish, Tommy croaker,
brown bait
RANGE & HABITAT
Most abundant from San Francisco
southward over sandy bottoms
LENGTH & WEIGHT
To 16+ in. and ~2 lb.
LIFE SPAN
To 15+ years
DIET & SUGGESTED BAIT
Eats fishes, squid, shrimp, octopus
worms, small crabs, clam. Use any
of these items for bait

Distinguishing Characteristics

Incandescent brownish to yellowish on the back becoming silvery below. Fins are yellow to white. Mouth beneath the head. No barbel. Twelve to 15 spines in the first dorsal fin.

Life History & Other Notes

White croakers eat a variety of fishes, squid, shrimp, octopus, worms, small crabs, clams and other items, living and dead.

Spawning may take place year-round, but most fish mature and spawn in the early spring months. Almost all females are believed to spawn more than once per season.

Although there is an unverified account of landing a four-pound white croaker, landing a fish that weighs in excess of two pounds is extremely rare. This fish can be caught on almost any kind of animal bait that is fished from piers or jetties over sandy or sand-mud bottoms. In fact, they are so easily hooked that anglers sometimes consider them a nuisance. A tough, difficult-to-steal bait such as squid is recommended.

105

Yellowfin Croaker

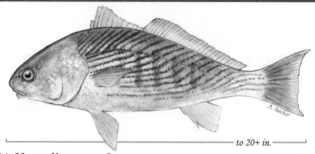

—— to 20+ in. ——

Yellowfin croaker are found south of Point Conception, California. They frequent bays, channels, harbors and other nearshore waters that have sand bottoms. These croakers are more abundant along beaches during the summer months and may move to deeper water in winter.

Distinguishing Characteristics

Iridescent blue to gray with brassy reflections on the back diffusing to silvery white below. Sides and back with many diagonal dark wavy lines. Fins are yellowish except for the dark dorsal fins. Body elliptical and elongate, with a somewhat arched back. Conical, blunt head. Single barbel. Two heavy spines at the front of the anal fin help to distinguish this croaker from the California corbina (which possesses one weak spine).

Life History & Other Notes

Yellowfin croaker eat mainly small fishes and fish fry, however invertebrates such as small crustaceans, worms, and mollusks are also eaten in large numbers.

Spawning takes place during the summer months when this species is most commonly found along sandy beaches. Maturity is apparently not reached until the fish are slightly over 9 inches long.

Yellowfin croakers are most often taken by surf anglers using soft-shelled sand crabs, worms, mussels, clams, or cut fish for bait. Like the California corbina and the spotfin croaker, this fish is reserved for sport fishermen – there is no commercial fishery for yellowfin croaker.

Yellowfin Croaker

SCIENTIFIC NAME
Umbrina roncador

OTHER COMMON NAMES
Catalina croaker, yellowtail croaker

RANGE & HABITAT
Point Conception south, over sand bottoms

LENGTH & WEIGHT
To 20+ in. and ~5 lb.

LIFE SPAN
To 10+ years

DIET & SUGGESTED BAIT
Eats small fishes, fish fry, small crustaceans, worms, mollusks. Try soft-shelled sand crabs, worms, mussels, clams or cut fish for bait

California Halibut

A. Bachar

— to 5 ft. —

California halibut may be found statewide in sandy and sand-mud environments. They have been found at depths of up to 300 ft., but are most abundant in waters less than 60 ft. deep. At times they are especially abundant in San Francisco Bay, and in the fast-running channels within Morro Bay and Mission Bay. At other times, they may be caught in the pounding surf along open, exposed beaches, or in areas with a mix of sand and rock bottom.

California Halibut

SCIENTIFIC NAME
Paralichthys californicus
OTHER COMMON NAMES
*flattie, chicken halibut,
barn door (larger fish)*
RANGE & HABITAT
Statewide in shallow, sandy areas
LENGTH & WEIGHT
To 5 ft. and 72 lb.
LIFE SPAN
To 30+ years
DIET & SUGGESTED BAIT/LURES
*Eats anchovies or other small fishes.
Try drift fishing with anchovies,
squid, queenfish, white croaker, or
shiner perch for bait, or try
artificial lures*

Distinguishing Characteristics

Brown to nearly black on the eyed side, and white on the blind side. Although a member of the left-eyed halibut family, California halibut are right-eyed over 40 percent of the time. Very large mouth, numerous teeth. Lateral line with high arch above the pectoral fin, on dark side.

Life History & Other Notes

California halibut feed almost exclusively on anchovies and similar small fishes. At times halibut are observed jumping clear of the water as they make passes at anchovy schooling near the surface.

Spawning takes place from April through July.

California halibut are pursued by anglers and spearfishers year-round. Fishing is generally best in the spring; however, in central and northern California fishing is especially good in summer and early fall when the halibut move in to shallow water to spawn.

Drifting for halibut is the most successful fishing method, using live anchovies, squid, white croakers, perch, or Pacific chub mackerel for bait. Artificial lures may also work well.

107

Diamond Turbot

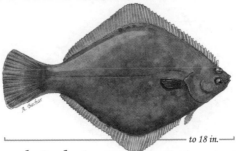

A. Bachar

to 18 in.

Diamond turbot are found south of Cape Mendocino off California, most commonly in quiet coastal waters, bays, and sloughs, on muddy or sandy bottoms often near some kind of structure. They are usually found in water depths ranging from four to 60 ft., but have been found at depths of over 150 ft.

Distinguishing Characteristics

Right-eyed. When freshly caught, eyed side is brownish green with pale blue spots; turns to near black after death. Blind side is white, with a yellow patch around mouth. Body diamond-shaped. Long dorsal branch of the lateral line.

Life History & Other Notes

Diamond turbot eat marine worms, clams, shrimps, crabs, and other small crustaceans. They are thought to reach sexual maturity in their second or third year, and spawn from September through February, with peak season between November and January. Individuals measuring between 12 and 15 inches long appear to be about eight to nine years old.

The diamond turbot is one of the most numerous fish in Southern California bays and sloughs.

Large numbers are taken using pieces of clams and shrimp (such as ghost shrimp) for bait. Their mouths are quite small, so hooks and light tackle are used. Mission, Newport, and San Francisco bays are important fishing areas for this species. They can be caught year-round, and will often put up a creditable fight for their size.

Although a challenge to prepare due to their small size and tough skin, many consider them excellent eating.

Diamond Turbot

SCIENTIFIC NAME
Hypsopsetta guttulata

RANGE & HABITAT
Cape Mendocino south, near shore especially in bays and sloughs over sandy or muddy bottom

LENGTH & WEIGHT
To 18 in. and 4 lb.

LIFE SPAN
To 8 years

DIET & SUGGESTED BAIT
Eats worms, clams, shrimps, crabs, and other small crustaceans. Try clams or ghost shrimp for bait.

Fantail Sole

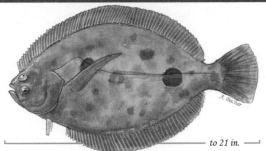

to 21 in.

The fantail sole
is a fairly rare inhabitant of sandy and muddy environments from Monterey Bay southward off California. This species inhabits 15 to 260 ft. depths and often buries itself in bottom sediments, as do many flatfishes.

Distinguishing Characteristics
Although a member of the left-eyed flounder family, this sole can be right-eyed. Uniform brown above, often with two dark spots, one near the pectoral fin, the other farther back on the lateral line. Young fish will have more spotting and mottling. High arch in the lateral line over the pectoral fin. Mouth small (does not reach the rear of lower eye); pectoral fin longer than head; tail fin rounded.

Life History & Other Notes
Fantail sole feed almost exclusively on crabs, but they will eat other small crustaceans, as well as worms and mollusks. They spawn throughout the year, with the most activity occurring in the latter half of the year from August through December. Young fantail sole swim in the water column until they change into their adult form and settle offshore on the bottom at depths of 66 to 135 ft. When first hatched the young swim upright; however, they soon start to turn on their left (or sometimes right) side and one eye migrates to the left (or sometimes right) side of their bodies.

Try using squid or clams to entice these fish to bite. Be sure to use hooks that will fit into their small mouths.

Fantail Sole
SCIENTIFIC NAME
Xystreurys liolepis
RANGE & HABITAT
Monterey Bay south on sandy or muddy bottoms
LENGTH
To 21 in.
DIET & SUGGESTED BAIT
Feeds on crabs & other crustaceans, also worms and mollusks. Squid and clams make good bait. Use small hooks.

109

Pacific Halibut

to 8+ ft.

The Pacific halibut ranges from Santa Rosa Island northward off California, but most are found north of Fort Bragg. They may be found at 20 to 3,600 ft. depths, and prefer deep, sandy bottom environments.

Distinguishing Characteristics

Right-eyed. Dark brown to black on the eyed side, white on blind side. Body elongate, rather slender, diamond-shaped. Corner of mouth forward of eye (in California halibut, the corner of mouth extends beyond the eye). Indented tail; high arch on lateral line over the pectoral fin.

Life History & Other Notes

The diet of the Pacific halibut includes fishes, crabs, clams, squid and other invertebrates.

Females become mature at 8 to 16 years of age (average 12); however males mature earlier. Spawning takes place from November through January. A large female weighing 140 lb. may produce more than 2½ million eggs. The eggs and young drift with the currents, gradually rising toward the surface as development proceeds. When first hatched, the young swim upright; however, they soon start to turn to their left side and the left eye migrates to the right side of their bodies. By early spring, the transformation is complete, and the young settle to the bottom in shallow waters.

Sport anglers in California usually catch smaller Pacific halibut than are available to the north. They are typically caught on crab, shrimp, squid, and other invertebrates.

Pacific Halibut

SCIENTIFIC NAME
Hippoglossus stenolepis

OTHER COMMON NAMES
northern halibut, right halibut, barn door (large fish)

RANGE & HABITAT
Santa Rosa Is. north; most common from Fort Bragg north, on deep sandy bottoms

LENGTH & WEIGHT
To 8+ ft. Males to 123 lb., females to 509 lb.

LIFE SPAN
To 42 years

DIET & SUGGESTED BAIT
Feeds on fishes (try sanddabs), crabs, clams, squid. Use heavy tackle

Sand Sole

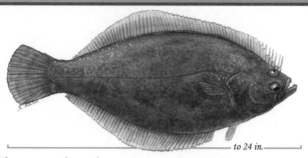

to 24 in.

The sand sole may

be found in sandy coastal environments and estuaries from Port Hueneme northward off California. They may range from 5 to 549 ft. depths, however they are generally found in shallow water, mostly in coastal bays, sloughs, and near-shore sandy areas. Young sand sole often found upstream of the Carquinez Strait, in Elkhorn Slough, and other, similar environments.

Sand Sole

SCIENTIFIC NAME
Psettichthys melanostictus
OTHER COMMON NAMES
sand flounder, fringe flounder
RANGE & HABITAT
*Port Hueneme north, in sandy
coastal environments*
LENGTH
To 24 in.
LIFE SPAN
To 10 years
DIET & SUGGESTED BAIT
*Feeds on fishes, worms, crustaceans
and mollusks. Try anchovy,
bloodworms, sand crab or
ghost shrimp for bait*

Distinguishing Characteristics

Right-eyed. Eyed side light green or gray to brown with fine, dark brown to black speckles. Blind side white. Dark skin feels like fine sandpaper. Dorsal and anal fins often with dull yellow on edges. Body elongate to oval. Tail fin rounded. Mouth and teeth large. First few dorsal fin rays long, mostly free of membrane.

Life History & Other Notes

Sand sole feed on fishes, worms, crustaceans and mollusks. They mature at 2 to 3 years, with females generally maturing a bit later than males. Sand sole spawn from January through July. The young swim in the water column until they change to adult form and settle on the bottom, usually in estuaries. Their left eye migrates to the right side of their bodies when they reach about 1 inch in length. Young sand sole feed on small crustaceans, marine worms, mollusks, and fish. The average foot-long sand sole is about five years old.

Sand sole may be caught from piers using anchovy, bloodworm, sand crab or ghost shrimp for bait. Their flesh is reputed to have a delicate flavor.

111

Sanddabs

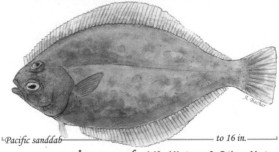

ᴸPacific sanddab ———————————— to 16 in. ———ᴵ

Four species of

sanddab are found in California waters: Pacific sanddab, longfin sanddab, speckled sanddab, and gulf sanddab. Most sport anglers catch the two largest sanddabs, the Pacific and the longfin. The Pacific sanddab is the predominant species in the California catch, with some longfin sanddab caught in Southern California. Longfin sanddabs range from Monterey Bay south, while Pacific sanddabs are caught statewide. Both species are found on muddy or sandy bottoms, generally at depths of from 30 to 600 ft., although Pacific sanddab are most abundant between 120 and 300 ft.

Distinguishing Characteristics

Left-eyed. Brown with white, orange, or yellow speckles. Pacific sanddab can be distinguished from longfin sanddab by the length of the pectoral fin on the eyed side: it is always shorter than the head on the Pacific sanddab and longer than the head on the longfin sanddab. In both, the lateral line is nearly straight for the length of the fish.

Life History & Other Notes

Both species eat a wide variety of prey, including small fishes, squid, octopus, fish eggs, shrimp, crabs and marine worms.

If you are fishing at the right depth, and the bottom is muddy or sandy, it can be difficult to keep sanddabs off the hook. Use small hooks baited with small pieces of squid or octopus. These two baits are tough and stay on the hook best, but small pieces of fish work equally well as bait.

Sanddabs

SCIENTIFIC NAMES
Citharichthys sordidus (Pacific)
Citharichthys xanthostigma (longfin)

OTHER COMMON NAMES
sand dab, soft flounder

RANGE & HABITAT
Pacific sanddab statewide; longfin sanddab from Monterey Bay south
Both on sandy or muddy bottoms

LENGTH & WEIGHT
Pacific sanddab to 16 in. and 2 lb.
Longfin sanddab to 10 in.

LIFE SPAN
Pacific sanddab to 10+ years

SUGGESTED BAIT
Try squid, fish or octopus for bait;
use small hooks

Starry Flounder

— to 3 ft. —

The starry flounder

inhabits sand, mud and gravel bottoms in coastal ocean waters, bays, sloughs, and even fresh water, from Santa Barbara northward off California. They may be found in extremely shallow water (only inches deep), to a maximum depth of 900 ft.

Distinguishing Characteristics

May be right- or left-eyed; the majority are left-eyed even though a member of the right-eyed flounder family. Dark brown on eyed side with alternating white to orange and black bars on the dorsal and anal fins; white on blind side. Body broad, relatively short, somewhat diamond shaped. Head short, eyes and mouth small; lower jaw slightly projecting. Large, rough, star-shaped scales on eyed side.

Life History & Other Notes

Starry flounders eat a wide variety of prey, including worms, crabs, clams, sand dollars, and brittle stars; large individuals may eat fishes, including sardines and sanddabs.

The spawning season extends from November through February. Spawning generally occurs in water shallower than 150 ft.

Like other flatfishes, the young are born with an eye on each side of the head. By the time they reach about ½ in. long, both eyes are on the same side and they resemble miniature versions of their parents.

Starry flounders are fairly numerous in central and northern California backwaters, particularly in San Francisco Bay. They are more frequently caught between December and March.

Starry Flounder

SCIENTIFIC NAME
Platichthys stellatus
OTHER COMMON NAMES
California flounder, rough jacket
RANGE & HABITAT
Santa Barbara northward, over sand, mud, gravel bottoms
LENGTH & WEIGHT
To 3 ft. and 20 lb.
LIFE SPAN
To 24 years
DIET & SUGGESTED BAIT
Feeds on worms, crabs, clams, fishes. Try using cut sardines, clams, shrimp, squid and worms for bait

113

Monkeyface Prickleback

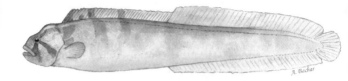

to 30 in.

Monkeyface pricklebacks are found statewide, but are most common north of Point Conception. They inhabit rock-pool areas between the high and low tide lines, seeking cover in crevices and secluded holes. Some favorite areas include the rocks north of Crescent City, between Bodega Bay and Dillon Beach, between Stinson Beach and Muir Beach, around the Golden Gate, and Shell Beach (near Pismo Beach). They are seldom seen moving in open waters.

Distinguishing Characteristics
Vary in color from dingy black to brownish-green. Two uniform stripes below eyes. Usually one or more reddish spots on side or belly. Long, eel-like body, no pelvic fins. Two spines in anal fin; large pectoral fins. Adult monkeyface pricklebacks, particularly breeding males, have a large fleshy lump on top of the head.

Life History & Other Notes
Despite their eel-like appearance, monkeyface pricklebacks are not in the eel family. They feed on plants such as sea lettuce, but may also take small shrimps or marine worms. Spawning takes place from

early January to early May. The tiny eggs are deposited on rocks formed into a ball and guarded by the parent. A ball of eggs about 3 inches in diameter may contain between 6,000 and 8,000 eggs.

Monkeyface pricklebacks are frequently taken by "poke-poling," a process where a long bamboo pole rigged with a wire leader and small baited hook on the end is inserted into likely crevices or cracks in the rocks, especially at low tide.

Monkeyface Prickleback

SCIENTIFIC NAME
Cebidichthys violaceus

OTHER COMMON NAMES
monkeyface eel

RANGE & HABITAT
Statewide, but most common north of Pt. Conception

LENGTH & WEIGHT
To 30 in. and 6+ lb.

LIFE SPAN
To 18+ years

DIET & SUGGESTED BAIT
Feeds on plants such as sea lettuce; also takes small shrimps or worms. Poke pole during the summer months with bait such as shrimp, mussels, clams, marine worms, fish

Wolf-Eel

A. Bachar

———— *to 6+ ft.* ————

The wolf-eel may

be found north of Imperial Beach, Southern California, from the intertidal zone to a depth of at least 740 ft. They are more common north of Point Conception.

Distinguishing Characteristics

Dark to light gray with darker and lighter mottling and circular patterns over entire body. Teeth large, doglike. Large pectoral fins; pelvic fins absent. Single, long dorsal fin.

Wolf-Eel

SCIENTIFIC NAME
Anarrhichthys ocellatus

OTHER COMMON NAMES
*mukah (Native American
for 'doctorfish')*

RANGE & HABITAT
*Imperial Beach north, more
common north of Pt. Conception in
rocky subtidal areas*

LENGTH & WEIGHT
To 6+ ft. and 41 lb.

DIET & SUGGESTED BAIT
*Feeds on crustaceans, sea urchins,
mussels, clams, some fishes. Use
shrimp, small crabs, squid, mussel,
or anchovy for bait; use heavy tackle*

Life History & Other Notes

Despite their eel-like bodies, wolf "eels" are not actually eels, but are related to blennies. They feed at night on sea urchins, mussels, crustaceans, clams, and some fishes. During the day, they rest in underwater rock crevices or caves.

Wolf-eels mature at around four years old, and may mate for life. Spawning season begins in October, and continues throughout the winter months. When mating, a pair of wolf-eels shares a rocky cave where the female lays her eggs. Both parents guard the eggs, with only one wolf-eel leaving the cave at a time until the eggs hatch several months later. The larvae and juveniles drift in the open ocean for up to two years before settling to rocky bottom habitat.

Wolf-eels may be caught using shrimp, small crabs, mussels, or anchovy. Because of the strength of their jaws and their habit of seeking rock refuges, use a stout hook (size 2/0) and 20- to 40-pound test fishing line; consider using a wire leader. They are a good-eating fish. Reportedly, some northwest Native American tribes reserved the wolf-eel for tribal healers.

115

Bocaccio

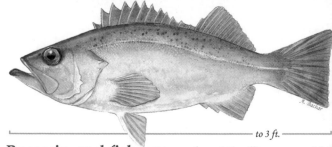

— to 3 ft. —

Bocaccio rockfish are

found statewide at depths of up to 1,050 ft. Juveniles can be found schooling around kelp beds or central California piers. When mature, they seek deeper water and begin to school near the bottom rather than near the surface. As adults, they are commonly found in waters from 250 to 750 ft. deep over fairly irregular, hard, or rocky bottom.

Distinguishing Characteristics

Brownish to dusky reddish extending down over the belly. Young fish are light bronze with speckling over the sides and back. Becomes darker & loses speckling with age. Body elongate, head pointed, mouth large, lower jaw greatly protruding. Upper jaw extends to behind eye.

Life History & Other Notes

Bocaccio feed mainly on fishes such as surfperch, jack mackerel, anchovies, and sardines. Squid, octopus and crab are also eaten.

Females mature at 17 in. long. As with all rockfish, fertilization is internal and development of the embryos takes place within the ovaries until the young are ready to hatch. A 28-inch female may produce 1.5 million young. Most young are born from December through April. Newly hatched young do not completely absorb the yolk from the egg stage for a period of 8 to 12 days.

Almost any rock or rubble bottom at depths from 250 to 750 ft. will yield bocaccio. Use baited hooks rigged above a sinker heavy enough to take the bait to the bottom on a fairly straight course. Because of the depths involved, a tough bait like squid is recommended.

Bocaccio

SCIENTIFIC NAME
Sebastes paucispinis
OTHER COMMON NAMES
salmon grouper, red snapper
RANGE & HABITAT
Statewide over rocky or hard bottom
LENGTH & WEIGHT
To 3 ft. and 21 lb.
LIFE SPAN
To 35+ years
DIET & SUGGESTED BAIT/LURES
Feeds on a wide variety of fishes, as well as squid, octopus and crab. Use squid for bait. Lures and jigs work well also

116

Black Rockfish

⊢————————————————— *to 27+ in.* ⊣

Black rockfish may

be found north of Paradise Cove off Southern California in a wide variety of habitats, including near the surface, on the bottom to depths of 1,200 ft., near rocky reefs, and in open water over deep banks or drop-offs. They frequently form loose schools 10 to 20 ft. above shallow (to 120 ft.) rocky reefs, in kelp beds, or in mid-water over deeper reefs (to 240 ft.), but individuals may also be found resting on rocky bottom.

Black Rockfish
SCIENTIFIC NAME
Sebastes melanops
OTHER COMMON NAMES
black snapper, black bass
RANGE & HABITAT
Statewide in a variety of habitats; uncommon south of Pt. Conception
LENGTH & WEIGHT
To 27+ in. and 10+ lb.
LIFE SPAN
To 50 years
DIET & SUGGESTED BAIT/LURES
Feeds on squid, crab eggs, fishes. Try cut fish, mussel, clam, crab, shrimp, or squid strips for bait. Some artificial lures including wet flies work as well

Distinguishing Characteristics

Brown to bluish-black on the back, paler on the sides, dirty white below. Continuous lighter band along lateral line. Body oval or egg-shaped; head with steep, almost straight upper profile; large mouth, lower jaw slightly projected. Black spots on the dorsal fin; anal fin rounded; upper jaw extends to rear of eye.

Life History & Other Notes

Black rockfish feed on squid, crab eggs, and various fishes. Like all rockfishes, fertilization and development of the embryos takes place within the body of the female. When development of the embryos is complete, the female releases the eggs. Exposure to sea water signals the embryos to escape from their egg cases.

These fish are commonly caught from commercial passenger fishing vessels, and incidentally when trolling for salmon. Rig a hook with almost any kind of cut fish bait. Mussel, clam, crab, shrimp and squid strips work almost equally as well, as do some kinds of wet flies and other artificial lures.

117

Black-and-Yellow Rockfish

— to 15+ in. —

Black-and-yellow rockfish may be found statewide, but they are uncommon north of Mendocino County and south of Point Conception. They range from intertidal depths to around 120 ft., but are most common in depths of 50 ft. or less.

Distinguishing Characteristics

Olive to black with yellow blotching and spotting; three or more light patches on upper half of body, extending onto dorsal fin and broken patches along lateral line. No continuous, lighter band along the lateral line. Body essentially the same shape as the gopher rockfish.

Life History & Other Notes

Black-and-yellow rockfish feed on crabs, shrimps, fishes including sculpins and rockfish, and squid.

As with all rockfish, fertilization is internal and development of the embryos takes place within the ovaries until the young are ready to hatch. The female then releases the eggs, and exposure to sea water signals the embryos to escape from their egg cases. Larval black-and-yellow rockfish drift with the currents until they are almost one inch long, when they take refuge in the upper canopies of kelp forests. As they grow, they move down the kelp until they reach their preferred rocky habitat at the bottom. Individual fish shelter in holes and crevices during the daytime, emerging at dusk. Black-and-yellow rockfish generally stake out home territories of at least 30 square feet.

Black-and-yellow rockfish may be taken in shallow water, and are often targeted by shore-based anglers using cut bait such as squid.

Black-and-Yellow Rockfish

SCIENTIFIC NAME
Sebastes chrysomelas

OTHER COMMON NAMES
black-and-yellow garrupa

RANGE & HABITAT
Statewide over rocky or hard bottom, especially between Pt. Conception & Sonoma County

LENGTH & WEIGHT
To 15+ in. and 3+ lb.

LIFE SPAN
To 30 years

DIET & SUGGESTED BAIT
Feeds on crabs, shrimps, small fishes and squid. Use cut or live bait

---

Blue Rockfish

— to 21 in. —

Blue rockfish are

found statewide off the California coast, especially north of Point Conception. They are most commonly caught from the surface to around 100 ft. depths, although they have been caught as deep as 300 ft. Large schools of blue rockfish may be found over rocky bottoms and around kelp beds.

Distinguishing Characteristics

Dark blue or olive brown to grayish black on the back, becoming lighter below; blotched with lighter shades on back and sides. No spots on dorsal fin; anal fin slanted; mouth extends only to mid-eye (these characteristics help to differentiate it from black rockfish). Five spines on gill cover.

Life History & Other Notes

Blue rockfish principally eat small fishes, shrimps and other crustaceans, and small pieces of algae or seaweed (the algae may be accidentally ingested while capturing other prey).

As with other rockfishes, fertilization is internal and live young are born. A 16-inch female may produce over half a million young. The main spawning season for blue rockfish runs from about November through March.

Blue rockfish may be caught in large quantities near rocky shores and around breakwaters, sunken ships, piles of rubble and similar locations along the California coast, especially north of Point Conception. They are caught just beneath the surface in and around kelp beds; where kelp is absent they live mostly near the bottom. Blue rockfish put up an excellent battle when hooked.

Blue Rockfish

SCIENTIFIC NAME
Sebastes mystinus

OTHER COMMON NAMES
blue bass, blue snapper

RANGE & HABITAT
Statewide, but especially north of Point Conception around rocky habitat & kelp beds

LENGTH & WEIGHT
To 21 in. and 3+ lb.

LIFE SPAN
To 44 years

DIET & SUGGESTED BAIT/LURES
Feeds on fishes & crustaceans. Try fishing with cut fish, mussels, clams, crab, shrimp, squid, wet flies or artificial lures

---

119

Brown Rockfish

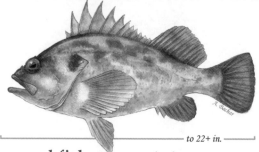

to 22+ in.

Brown rockfish may

be found statewide off the California coast. They occur most commonly from very shallow nearshore waters, such as bays, to around 400 ft. depths, although they have been found as deep as 450 ft.

Distinguishing Characteristics

Various shades of brown, overlaid with dark brown, red-brown or black mottling. Prominent dark blotch on rear gill cover, fainter in large fish. Red-brown, brown, or orange-ish stripes radiate back from eyes and upper jaw. Heavy-bodied. Fins pinkish.

Life History & Other Notes

Brown rockfish feed on various small invertebrates such as crabs and shrimp, as well as small fishes.

Fertilization is internal, as with most rockfishes, and development of the embryos takes place within the female's ovaries until the young are ready to hatch. The female then releases the eggs, and exposure to sea water signals the embryos that it is time to escape from their egg cases. Juvenile brown rockfish drift with the currents for up to three months, and settle in rocky shallow water habitat, near bits of drift kelp

at the bottom, or on submarine canyon walls. Bays may be an important nursery area for this species. Adults are solitary or live in small groups in deeper waters near rocky outcroppings, often with vermilion, copper, canary, and calico rockfishes.

Brown rockfish may be caught using mussel, clam, crab, shrimp or squid strips for bait, or try using wet flies or other artificial lures.

Brown Rockfish

SCIENTIFIC NAME
Sebastes auriculatus

OTHER COMMON NAMES
bolina cod, chocolate bass

RANGE & HABITAT
Statewide over rocky or hard bottom

LENGTH & WEIGHT
To 22+ in. and 5+ lb.

LIFE SPAN
To 34 years

DIET & SUGGESTED BAIT/LURES
Feeds on crabs, shrimps, and small fishes. Try mussels, clams, crab, shrimp, or squid for bait. May also take wet flies or other artificial lures.

California Scorpionfish

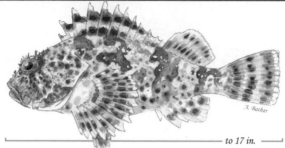

A. Bachar

⊢———————————————— to 17 in. ———⊣

California scorpionfish,

commonly known as *sculpin*, are found off the coast of California from Santa Cruz southward. Most are caught over hard, rocky bottoms at depths ranging from just below the surface to 600 ft., but some may occasionally be taken over sand or mud bottoms.

Distinguishing Characteristics

Red to brown with dark blotches and spotting over body and fins. Stocky body with large, spiny head, mouth, and pectoral fins.

California Scorpionfish

SCIENTIFIC NAME
Scorpaena guttata

OTHER COMMON NAMES
sculpin, rattlesnake

RANGE & HABITAT
Santa Cruz southward, mostly south of Pt. Conception, over rocky or other hard bottom habitat

LENGTH & WEIGHT
To 17 in. and 3+ lb.

LIFE SPAN
To 21 years

DIET & SUGGESTED BAIT
Feeds on crab, squid, octopus, fishes, and shrimp. Try cut fish or squid for bait, or artificial lures

Life History & Other Notes

California scorpionfish feed on crab, squid, octopus, fishes, and shrimp.

Spawning season takes place from April through August. California scorpionfish eggs are embedded in the gelatinous walls of hollow, pear-shaped egg balloons. The paired egg balloons, each 5 to 10 in. long, are joined at the small ends and contain a single layer of eggs. These transparent-to-greenish egg balloons rise rapidly from the bottom of the ocean to the surface, and release the young fish after about five days.

The California scorpionfish is the most venomous member of the scorpionfish family off California. Its dorsal, pelvic and anal fin spines possess venom glands, and are capable of inflicting very painful wounds. Immediate immersion of the wound in very hot water seems to bring the best relief.

California scorpionfish readily take a hook baited with squid or fish. To remove the hook safely, insert your thumb into the mouth and grip the lower jaw firmly between your thumb and fingers while removing the hook.

121

Chilipepper

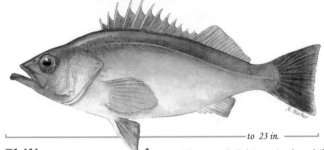

— to 23 in. —

Chilipepper may be
found statewide off the California coast. They are a deepwater rockfish, and prefer rocky bottom habitat. They are generally found at depths greater than 300 ft., but have been caught at a depths of up to 1,080 ft.

Distinguishing Characteristics
Pinkish, becoming whitish below. Lateral line is lighter, and bright red. Body slender and rather elongate. Head elongate, pointed, with few spines. Lower jaw projects beyond upper. Upper jaw extends only to about the center of the eye, not past it as with bocaccio. Mouth generally smaller than bocaccio.

Life History & Other Notes
Adult chilipepper feed on small crustaceans, small squid, and small fishes including anchovies, young hake, small sardines, and lantern-fishes.

As with other rockfishes, fertilization is internal and live young are born. The number of young a female may produce increases with size; for example, a 12-inch female may produce 29,000 young, while a 22-inch female may produce over half a million young.

122

The usual fishing rig for chilipepper includes a baited hook above a sinker that is heavy enough to take the line to the bottom on a fairly straight course. Chilipepper are often fished in mid-water as well as on the bottom. Because of the depths involved, it may take quite a while to lower and raise the rig, therefore the bait should be tough enough to remain on the hook. Squid or salted anchovies are ideal.

Chilipepper
SCIENTIFIC NAME
Sebastes goodei
OTHER COMMON NAMES
chili, red snapper
RANGE & HABITAT
Statewide in rocky, deepwater habitat
LENGTH & WEIGHT
To 23 in. and 5+ lb.
LIFE SPAN
To 35 years
DIET & SUGGESTED BAIT
Feeds on small crustaceans, small squid, small fishes. Try using squid, salted cut anchovies, or fish flesh with skin still attached for bait

Copper Rockfish

— to 26+ in. —

Copper rockfish are

found statewide off the California coast, but are most common from the Santa Barbara Channel Islands and Southern California coast to central California. Generally speaking, copper rockfish may be found from the intertidal area (especially very young individuals) to water depths around 600 ft.

Distinguishing Characteristics

Highly variable in color. Wide range of blotchy colors; commonly olive, dark brown, copper-pink, or red. Light-colored strip along rear two-thirds of lateral line. Several bars radiate back from eyes. Belly bright white. Deep red individuals that may be mistaken for vermilion rockfish are frequently found around the Channel Islands.

Life History & Other Notes

Copper rockfish usually feed during morning and evening hours near the bottom on crabs, shrimps, and other crustaceans. They will also eat squid, octopus, spiny dogfish, and small fishes including greenlings and surfperches.

As with other rockfishes, fertilization is internal and live young are born. Young copper rockfish are usually found over sand or low rock features. Adults are primarily found in boulder fields and over larger rocks, where they may be solitary or gathered in aggregations of up to 100 individuals.

This fish is often taken with other rockfish species including gopher, vermilion and black rockfishes. It will readily bite cut strips of squid, live bait such as anchovies, and various jigs.

Copper Rockfish

SCIENTIFIC NAME
Sebastes caurinus

OTHER COMMON NAMES
whitebelly, chucklehead, neverdies

RANGE & HABITAT
Statewide, more offshore in Southern California, over rocky habitat

LENGTH
To 26+ in.

LIFE SPAN
To 50 years

DIET & SUGGESTED BAIT/LURES
Feeds on crab, squid, octopus, fishes, and shrimp. Try fishing with squid or live anchovies for bait, or use jigs

---

123

Gopher Rockfish

to 17 in.

Most gopher rockfish

are caught between Pt. Conception and Monterey Bay in nearshore waters, but they may generally be found from Mendocino County southward off California. Gopher rockfish range from the intertidal zone to depths of around 260 ft., but are most commonly found at depths greater than 40 ft.

Distinguishing Characteristics

Olive brown to reddish brown, with three or more light patches on the upper half extending into the dorsal fin. Broken light patches along the lateral line; no light-colored strip along the lateral line. Spiny head. Body shape essentially the same as the black-and-yellow rockfish.

Life History & Other Notes

Gopher rockfish feed on crabs, shrimps, fishes including sculpins and small rockfish, and squid.

As with all rockfish, fertilization is internal and development of the embryos takes place within the ovaries until the embryos are ready to hatch. When the female releases the eggs, exposure to sea water causes the embryos to escape from their egg cases. Larval gopher rockfish drift with the currents until they are nearly an inch long, when they take refuge in upper kelp canopies. As they grow, they move down the kelp until they reach their preferred rocky habitat at the bottom. Individual fish shelter in holes and crevices during the daytime, emerging at dusk.

This fish is often taken with other rockfish species including black-and-yellow and vermilion rockfishes.

Gopher Rockfish

SCIENTIFIC NAME
Sebastes carnatus

OTHER COMMON NAMES
gopher cod, butterball

RANGE & HABITAT
Statewide over rocky or hard bottom, but uncommon north of Sonoma County

LENGTH
To 17 in.

LIFE SPAN
To 35 years

DIET & SUGGESTED BAIT/LURES
Feeds on crabs, shrimps, small fishes and squid. Try fishing with squid or live anchovies, or try jigs

---

Grass Rockfish

to 22 in.

Grass rockfish may be caught statewide near shore. They live in very shallow waters among seaweeds, kelp, and rocky reefs, often where caves and crevices are common, although they may also be found over small boulder fields as well. The average depth at which grass rockfish may be caught is about 15 ft., but they are more abundant at a depth of 30 ft. Grass rockfish have been found at a depth of up to 150 ft.

Grass Rockfish

SCIENTIFIC NAME
Sebastes rastrelliger
OTHER COMMON NAMES
grass bass
RANGE & HABITAT
Statewide in very shallow waters, near kelp over rocky bottom
LENGTH
To 22 in.
LIFE SPAN
To 23 years
DIET & SUGGESTED BAIT
Feeds on crab, shrimps, snails, small fishes. Try using stripbaits, mussel, clam, or shrimp for bait, presented on the bottom

Distinguishing Characteristics

Blackish green to olive green with paler green or brown mottling. Very rarely orange. Pectoral fins usually have pink edges (when freshly caught). Pectoral fin rays thick and fleshy. May have blackish blotch on the posterior part of the gill cover. Body heavy, stubby, spiny. Very short, blunt gillrakers on the first gill arch (lift gill cover to observe gill rakers).

Life History & Other Notes

Grass rockfish are probably most active at night. They feed on bottom-dwelling creatures such as crabs, shrimps, snails, and small fishes such as sea perch.

As with all rockfish, fertilization is internal and development of the embryos takes place within the ovaries until the young are ready to hatch. When the female releases the eggs, exposure to sea water causes the embryos to escape from their egg cases. Spawning takes place during the winter months and the young are found from March to September in the same areas as adults.

Stripbaits, mussels, clams or shrimps will all entice grass rockfish to bite.

125

Kelp Rockfish

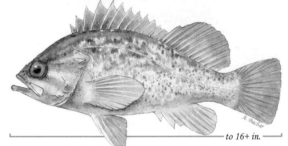

— to 16+ in. —

Kelp rockfish are found from Albion in Mendocino County southward off the coast of California. They may be found in kelp beds and among rocks from the surface to 140 ft., but are most abundant at depths averaging about 35 ft.

Distinguishing Characteristics

Drab olive-gray to olive-brown, most commonly light tan or brown. Head and dorsal area often darker than rest of body. Spiny head, comparatively large pectoral fins. May be distinguished from brown rockfish by its lack of a dark spot on the gill cover; may be distinguished from grass rockfish by observing the gill rakers, which are long and slender (lift gill cover to observe gill rakers).

Life History & Other Notes

Kelp rockfish feed mostly at night on small crustaceans, shrimps and small fishes.

As with all rockfish, fertilization is internal and development of the embryos takes place within the ovaries until they are ready to hatch. The female releases the eggs, and exposure to sea water causes the embryos to escape from their egg cases. Kelp rockfish release their larvae from March through June off central California. They settle at an early age into kelp forest habitat, although they are also abundant around some nearshore oil platforms in the Santa Barbara Channel.

Kelp rockfish may be taken from the rocks or in offshore kelp beds using live bait, fish strips, mussels, clams, shrimp, or squid. They may also be taken on occasion using metallic lures.

Kelp Rockfish

SCIENTIFIC NAME
Sebastes atrovirens
OTHER COMMON NAMES
sugar bass
RANGE & HABITAT
*Albion south, in kelp beds
& rocky environments*
LENGTH & WEIGHT
To 16+ in.
LIFE SPAN
To 25 years
DIET & SUGGESTED BAIT/LURES
Feeds on crustaceans, shrimps, small fishes. Try using live bait, fish strips, mussels, clams, shrimps, or squid for bait. May also be taken with artificial lures

Olive Rockfish

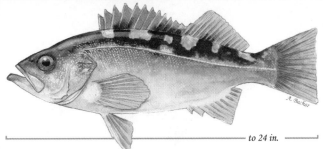

to 24 in.

Olive rockfish are

found from Crescent City southward off California, but are rarely caught north of Fort Bragg. This shallow-water species lives near the surface in and around kelp beds and near the bottom in rocky areas where the kelp does not form dense beds that reach the surface. They are especially common around kelp beds where the water is 40 ft. deep or deeper, and have been caught at depths as great as 480 ft.

Olive Rockfish

SCIENTIFIC NAME
Sebastes serranoides
OTHER COMMON NAMES
johnny bass, jonathan
RANGE & HABITAT
Fort Bragg southward in shallow waters, near eelgrass or kelp over rocky bottom
LENGTH
To 24 in.
LIFE SPAN
To 30 years
DIET & SUGGESTED BAIT / LURES
Feeds on fishes, squid, octopus, shrimps, and marine worms. Try live anchovy for bait, or a artificial lures presented on the bottom

Distinguishing Characteristics

Usually dark olive- or greenish-gray with lighter blotches on the back, color lightens on the sides. Color varies from olive green to bright yellow. No red-brown flecking on scales (lack of flecking helps to differentiate olive rockfish from yellowtail rockfish). Almost no head spines, except for spines on the gill cover (gill cover spines help differentiate olive rockfish from kelp bass). Body streamlined.

Life History & Other Notes

Olive rockfish feed mainly on fishes, but will also take shrimps, squid, octopus, and marine worms. They live over rugged rocky areas, as well as at mid-water, especially around offshore oil platforms. They are a schooling fish, forming small- to moderate-sized schools, often with blue or black rockfish. Young olive rockfish may settle near kelp beds, oil platforms, surf grass or other suitable habitat in depths as shallow as 10 ft.

Kelp beds along the mainland shore usually yield olive rockfish, but the best fishing may be had around San Nicholas or Santa Barbara Islands. Olive rockfish are great fighters.

127

Quillback Rockfish

to 24 in.

Quillback rockfish

are found from Point Sur northward off California, but they are most common off northern California. This fish may be found in subtidal areas to depths of around 900 ft. Quillback rockfish are bottom dwellers, and prefer rocky areas and/or kelp cover.

Distinguishing Characteristics

Brown with yellowish to orange blotches toward the front of the body. Light-colored "saddle patches" extending over the head and through the spiny dorsal fin. Head spiny; may have orange to brown speckling extending back over body to just past the pectoral fins. Dorsal fin spines very long, membranes between the spines deeply incised. Fins dark brown to black, except where dorsal fin is blotched.

Life History & Other Notes

Quillback rockfish are primarily bottom feeders that prey on crustaceans, but they will take small fishes in the water column occasionally. They are believed to feed mostly during morning and evening hours.

As with all rockfish, fertilization is internal. Development of the embryos takes place within the ovaries until the young are ready to hatch. When the female releases her eggs, exposure to sea water causes the embryos to escape from the egg cases. Young are released off central and northern California from April through July.

Quillback rockfish may be taken from the rocks or in offshore kelp beds using crabs, shrimp, or squid for bait.

Quillback Rockfish

SCIENTIFIC NAME
Sebastes maliger

OTHER COMMON NAMES
brown bomber

RANGE & HABITAT
Point Sur northward, mostly off northern California in rocky areas with kelp cover

LENGTH
To 24 in.

LIFE SPAN
To 95 years

DIET & SUGGESTED BAIT
Feeds on crustaceans and small fishes. Try using crabs, shrimps, squid, or live anchovies for bait and artificial lures

Starry Rockfish

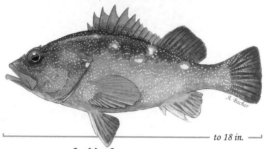

to 18 in.

Starry rockfish, named for the small, star-like spots scattered over their bodies, are found from Cordell Bank southward off California. They prefer rocky offshore reefs at 80 to 900 ft. depths.

Distinguishing Characteristics
Red-orange, profusely covered with small white spots. Four or five large whitish blotches along back. Body elongate, robust and heavy towards the front. Head pointed in profile; large mouth, lower jaw projects slightly beyond upper jaw when mouth is closed.

Life History & Other Notes
Starry rockfish feed on shrimps, crabs and small fishes such as anchovies. They are solitary animals, and rarely rise more than three feet off the sea floor.

As with all rockfish, fertilization is internal. Development of the embryos takes place within the ovaries until the young are ready to hatch. When the female releases her eggs, exposure to sea water causes the embryos to escape from their egg cases. A female starry rockfish may release between 33,000 and 228,000 young per year, usually between March and May.

Starry rockfish may be caught in conjunction with vermilion, rosy, greenspotted and greenstriped rockfish. The usual fishing rig for starry rockfish consists of baited hooks above a sinker heavy enough to take the line to the bottom on a fairly straight course. Because of the depths fished, the bait should be sufficiently tough to remain firmly on the hook while being nibbled and chewed upon by the quarry. Cut squid is ideal.

Starry Rockfish

SCIENTIFIC NAME
Sebastes constellatus

OTHER COMMON NAMES
spotted corsair, red snapper

RANGE & HABITAT
*Cordell Bank south
over rocky offshore reefs*

LENGTH & WEIGHT
To 18 in.

LIFE SPAN
To 32 years

DIET & SUGGESTED BAIT
*Feeds on shrimps, crabs,
and small fishes.
Try squid for bait, and
artificial lures*

129

Treefish

to 16 in.

Treefish are rockfish

whose Latin species name *serriceps* means "saw head," in reference to the fish's prominent head spines. The treefish may be found from San Francisco southward off California, but is uncommon north of Point Conception. They inhabit very shallow nearshore waters to depths of 320 ft., but are most frequently found above 200 ft. They prefer rugged, rocky areas with lots of crevices and caves, where they often hide.

Distinguishing Characteristics
Body color yellow to greenish-yellow, with five to six black, brown, or dark green vertical bars. Two oblique bars radiate back from eyes. Red, pink, or orange lips. Heavy head spines. May have tiny, lighter-colored specks on body.

Life History & Other Notes
Like the starry rockfish, this is a solitary fish. Treefish prey on shrimps, crabs, and fishes, and are believed to hunt their quarry at dusk or under the cover of nightfall.

As with all rockfish, fertilization is internal. Development of the embryos takes place within the ovaries until the young are ready to hatch. When the female releases her eggs, exposure to sea water causes the embryos to escape from their egg cases. Young treefish are known to be released during June and July.

Treefish are often caught over shallow reefs, particularly from Point Conception southward. They are targeted by anglers using cut bait such as squid, but may also be taken using live fish for bait, or lures.

Treefish
SCIENTIFIC NAME
Sebastes serriceps
OTHER COMMON NAMES
lipstick bass, barber pole
RANGE & HABITAT
Mostly Pt. Conception southward over fairly shallow rocky areas
LENGTH & WEIGHT
To 16 in.
LIFE SPAN
To 23 years
DIET & SUGGESTED BAIT
Feeds on crustaceans and small fishes. Try using crabs, shrimps, or squid for bait, and artificial lures

---

Vermilion Rockfish

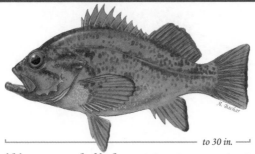

to 30 in.

Vermilion rockfish are found throughout California waters near rugged, rocky areas and towards the bottom of oil platforms near shell mounds and pipelines. They may be caught at depths between 50 and 500 ft. (usually less than 100 ft. off central California), although they have been taken from depths as great as 900 ft.

Distinguishing Characteristics
Bright red on body and fins, black and gray mottling on young fish.

Fish less than 12 inches long may have black-edged fins. Body moderately deep. Upper profile of head moderately curved, large mouth, lower jaw slightly projecting. Weak head spines. Underside of jaw feels rough when rubbed from tail to head.

Life History & Other Notes
Vermilion rockfish feed almost exclusively on fishes, squid and octopus.

Vermilion rockfish appear to mature and spawn for the first time when they are 3 to 4 years old. Fertilization is internal and they give birth to live young. A female measuring 20 inches long was estimated to contain 282,000 eggs. By this measure, a 30-inch fish may contain as many as half a million eggs. Most spawning takes place from December through March.

The vermilion rockfish is a very popular and highly sought-after fish. The usual fishing rig consists of baited hooks above a sinker heavy enough to take the line to the bottom on a fairly straight course. A lot of baiting time can be saved by using a tough, difficult-to-steal bait such as a piece of squid or salted mackerel.

Vermilion Rockfish

SCIENTIFIC NAME
Sebastes miniatus

OTHER COMMON NAMES
red snapper, red rock cod

RANGE & HABITAT
*Statewide over rocky reefs
or other structure*

LENGTH & WEIGHT
To 30 in. and 15+ lb.

LIFE SPAN
To 60 years

DIET & SUGGESTED BAIT
*Feeds on fishes, squid and octopus.
Try using live squid and anchovies,
or salted mackerel for bait, and
artificial lures such as leadhead jigs,
swimbaits, and diamond bars.*

Yellowtail Rockfish

— to 26 in. —

Yellowtail rockfish may be found from San Diego northward, however they are most frequently caught off central and northern California. They are often found over deep reefs from the surface down to 1,800 ft. Yellowtail rockfish usually swim well off the bottom in schools that sometimes contain thousands of fish that also include vermilion and canary rockfish, but have been known to rest on the bottom in rocky caves and crevices as well.

Distinguishing Characteristics

Grayish-brown above, shading into white below. Sides finely spotted with yellow. Tail yellow, fins dusky yellow. Red-brown flecking on side scales helps differentiate this species from the olive rockfish. Convex profile between eyes; no spines on top of head, lower jaw projects outwards. Anal fin slants vertically.

Life History & Other Notes

Yellowtail rockfish feed on small Pacific whiting, anchovy, lanternfish and other small fishes, as well as on small squid and shrimps.

As with other rockfishes, fertilization is internal and live young are born. The number of developing eggs increases with the female's size; a fish 19 to 21 inches long may produce 633,000 eggs.

When fishing for yellowtail rockfish in deep water, the usual fishing rig consists of baited hooks above a sinker heavy enough to take the line to the bottom on a fairly straight course. Since this species occurs quite often near the surface, standard mid-water fishing techniques and baits, and small silvery lures or small plastic jigs should also work well.

Yellowtail Rockfish

SCIENTIFIC NAME
Sebastes flavidus

OTHER COMMON NAMES
yellowtail, yellow bass

RANGE & HABITAT
San Diego northward, but mostly off central and Southern California over rocky reefs

LENGTH & WEIGHT
To 26 in. and 7+ lb.

LIFE SPAN
To 64 years

DIET & SUGGESTED BAIT/LURES
Feeds on fishes, squid, shrimp. Try using these for bait, also lures including jigs and flies fished off the bottom

Cabezon

to 39 in.

C a b e z o n m a y b e encountered anywhere along the California coast where there are rugged rocks and kelp beds. They prefer shallow waters less than 100 ft. deep, although they are known to occur as deep as 250 ft. This popular fish is caught frequently in central and northern California.

Distinguishing Characteristics

Usually dark brown with mottling, but color varies from blue-green to bright red. Body elongate and stout. Head large and broad; snout bluntly rounded. Large mouth with pale to dark blue lining. No scales anywhere on body; small flap of skin (called a *cirrus*) over each eye and in the middle of the snout. Pectoral fins large with fleshy rays.

Life History & Other Notes

The cabezon diet includes mollusks (especially abalone), fishes, and crabs.

Female cabezon grow faster and attain larger sizes than do males. Spawning takes place from November through March, peaking in January. Adults congregate at nesting sites to lay large masses of eggs on cleared rocks. The nest is guarded by the male, who will drive away any intruder.

Suitable baits include abalone trimmings, mussels, clams, squid, shrimp, worms, cut or strip bait, and live bait. Cabezon are bottom dwellers, and can be most difficult to land if allowed to retreat to the shelter of rocks or seaweeds after being hooked.

Cabezon eggs are poisonous and can cause severe illness if eaten. Cabezon flesh, on the other hand, is harmless and quite tasty.

Cabezon

SCIENTIFIC NAME
Scorpaenichthys marmoratus
OTHER COMMON NAMES
bullhead, cabby, cabezone
RANGE & HABITAT
Statewide on nearshore reefs
LENGTH & WEIGHT
To 39 in. and 25 lb.
LIFE SPAN
To 17 years
DIET & SUGGESTED BAIT
Feeds on crabs, mollusks, and fishes. Try abalone trimmings, mussels, clams, squid, shrimp, worms, cut bait, strip bait, or live baitfish, and artificial lures

133

Kelp Greenling, Rock Greenling

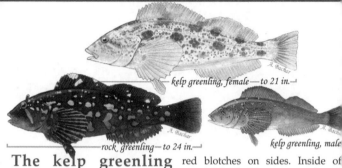

kelp greenling, female— to 21 in.

A. Bachar

rock greenling— to 24 in.

A. Bachar

kelp greenling, male

A. Bach

The kelp greenling and rock greenling are very closely related. Kelp greenling are most common in central and northern California. They may be found southward to La Jolla, but are quite rare south of Point Conception. Rock greenling may be found southward to Point Conception, but are rare south of San Francisco. Both species prefer relatively shallow water habitats along rocky coasts, around jetties, and in kelp beds, and so probably compete directly for space and food. The maximum recorded depth for kelp greenling is 150 ft.

Distinguishing Characteristics
Male kelp greenling: Dark gray to brown, front half with numerous sky-blue spots, each surrounded by a ring of rust-colored spots. Very small flap of skin (*cirrus*) over each eye and halfway to the dorsal fin. **Female kelp greenling**: Gray-brown, uniformly covered with round reddish-brown spots. Inside of mouth yellowish. Very small cirrus over each eye and halfway to the dorsal fin. **Rock greenling (both sexes)**: Reddish-brown with darker mottling, often with large bright-

red blotches on sides. Inside of mouth bluish. Cirrus over each eye.

Life History & Other Notes
Both kelp and rock greenlings feed on various sea worms, crustaceans, and small fishes. They can be caught using cut pieces of fish, clams, mussels, shrimp, squid, worms and crab backs for bait, or try feathered jigs tipped with squid. Once hooked, greenlings can be difficult to land because of their habit of entangling anglers' lines in rocks or kelp.

Kelp Greenling & Rock Greenling

SCIENTIFIC NAME
Hexagrammos decagrammus (kelp)
Hexagrammos lagocephalus (rock)

OTHER COMMON NAMES
sea trout, rock trout, kelp trout

RANGE & HABITAT
Most frequently in central and northern California, in rocky habitats and kelp forests

LENGTH
Kelp greenling: To 21 in.
Rock greenling: To 24 in.

LIFE SPAN
Kelp greenling: To 16 years
Rock greenling: To 11 years

Lingcod

blue-green color variation

— to 45 in. —

Lingcod may be found statewide off California. This fish lives at or near the bottom, in a wide range of habitats including rocky areas and kelp beds, especially where there is strong tidal movement. They occur most abundantly in water shallower than 350 ft., but will often go into deeper water and have been caught as deep as 2,700 ft. off Southern California.

Distinguishing Characteristics

Generally dark brown, but varies from blue-green to red-brown, with many spots and blotches on the upper part of the body. Body and head elongate, head conical, mouth large with many sharp teeth.

Life History & Other Notes

Although young lingcod feed primarily on shrimps and other crustaceans, adults eat fishes, squid and octopus.

Spawning usually takes place from December through March. The large, adhesive egg masses are often laid in rocky crevices on sub-tidal reefs. The male lingcod guards the eggs until they hatch. A 45-inch female can lay an average of half a million eggs in a single season.

Lingcod are easily caught using standard rockfish rigs baited with anchovies or squid pieces. Larger bait such as live squid, mackerel, sanddabs or small rockfishes will often produce very large lingcod.

Lingcod teeth and gillrakers are very sharp and can cause serious injury. Pick up legal-sized fish safely by grasping the eye socket(s) with one hand, and the tail with the other. Always net undersized fish to return them safely to the water.

Lingcod

SCIENTIFIC NAME
Ophiodon elongatus
OTHER COMMON NAMES
green ling, slinky linky, lingasaur
RANGE & HABITAT
Statewide over rocky reefs and kelp beds
LENGTH & WEIGHT
To 45 in. and 54 lb.
LIFE SPAN
To 25 years
DIET & SUGGESTED BAIT/LURES
Feeds on all types of fishes, squid, octopus. Try live anchovies, sardines, sanddabs, or squid for bait, or metal or plastic jigs

135

Barred Sand Bass

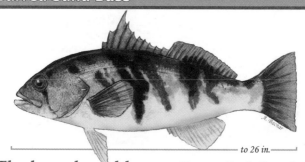

to 26 in.

The barred sand bass may be found from Santa Cruz southward off California to a depth of 600 ft.; however, most fish are taken in 60 to 90 ft. of water. They are usually found near the sand/rock interfaces of deeper reefs and artificial submerged structures.

Distinguishing Characteristics
Dark gray to greenish; gray-white on back, white on belly, dark vertical bars on sides; no spots. Body elongate, mouth large; lower jaw protrudes slightly. Third dorsal spine, the longest of the dorsal spines, is much longer than first two dorsal fin spines.

Life History & Other Notes
The barred sand bass diet includes crabs, octopus, squid, and small fishes.

Adult barred sand bass gather to spawn during the warm summer months. Their eggs are free-floating, and striped young appear in Southern California nearshore areas and eelgrass beds during fall and winter.

Most barred sand bass landed in California are taken between May and October. They are fished in three main areas: Horseshoe Kelp to Newport Beach, Dana Point to Oceanside, and the Silver Strand off San Diego.

Barred sand bass are reserved only for sport fishermen (no commercial fishery exists). The best method for catching this fish is to search a sandy area with a fishfinder until a school is located. Anchor the boat and offer live anchovy for bait. If you chum with anchovy, barred sand bass will usually gather under the boat; thus it pays to wait awhile before moving to a different spot.

Barred Sand Bass
SCIENTIFIC NAME
Paralabrax nebulifer
OTHER COMMON NAMES
sand bass, ground bass, sandy
RANGE & HABITAT
Santa Cruz southward off rocky reefs and artificial structure
LENGTH & WEIGHT
To 26 in. and ~11 lb.
LIFE SPAN
To 24 years
DIET & SUGGESTED BAIT/LURES
Feeds on crabs, squid, octopus, and small fishes. Try using live anchovies for bait and artificial lures

Kelp Bass

⊢——————— *to ~28 in.* ——⊣

Although they may be caught infrequently in northern California, kelp bass are a mainstay for sport fishermen south of Point Conception. They are typically found in shallow water (surface to 150 ft.) near rugged, rocky reefs, kelp beds, or other structure. They seem to prefer water depths between 8 and 70 ft.

Distinguishing Characteristics

Brown to olive-green with light blotches, becoming lighter below.

Kelp Bass

SCIENTIFIC NAME
Paralabrax clathratus

OTHER COMMON NAMES
calico bass, bull bass

RANGE & HABITAT
*Statewide, but mostly
south of Pt. Conception over
rocky reefs and in kelp beds*

LENGTH & WEIGHT
To ~28 in. and ~14 lb.

LIFE SPAN
To 34 years

DIET & SUGGESTED BAIT/LURES
*Feeds on shrimp-like crustaceans
and fish. Try anchovies for bait,
or artificial lures such as plugs,
spoons, jigs, and flies*

Body and head elongate, pointed snout. Large mouth. Third, fourth and fifth dorsal spines all about the same length. No gill cover spines.

Life History & Other Notes

Small, shrimp-like crustaceans are very important in the diet of kelp bass of all ages. Larger kelp bass also eat small fishes such as anchovies and small surfperch.

The spawning season usually extends from May through September with a peak during July. As with most members of the marine bass family, kelp bass are slow-growing. A fish 16½ inches long may be about 9 years old.

The kelp bass is a very popular sport fish, reserved only for sport fishermen (no commercial fishery exists). They are caught primarily with live anchovies fished near the surface in and around kelp beds. They may be taken throughout the water column by trolling near kelp beds with live or dead bait. Numerous anglers also catch them on plugs, spoons, lures, and jigs. Kelp bass are noted for their fighting qualities, regardless of the type of bait or lure used.

137

Spotted Sand Bass

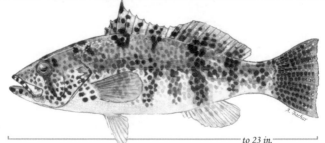

to 23 in.

The spotted sand bass

may be found from Monterey southward off California to a depth of 200 ft.; however, this species is generally confined to large bays in Southern California. In fact, it is rarely seen north of Santa Monica Bay. Because of their preference for bays, spotted sand bass are taken less frequently than kelp bass or barred sand bass, which are found on the open coast. Within bays, spotted sand bass prefer muddy or sandy areas of eelgrass or surf grass, as well as underwater structure such as rocks or pilings.

Distinguishing Characteristics

Olive brown with round black spots on body, head and fins. No vertical bars on sides. Body moderately elongate; mouth large, bottom jaw protrudes slightly. Third dorsal fin spine is much longer than first two dorsal fin spines, and is the longest of the dorsal spines. Spawning males: white lower jaw and overall high contrast body coloration. Spawning females: yellow lower jaw and darker body coloration.

Life History & Other Notes

Spotted sand bass mainly consume crustaceans, clams, and small fishes.

Spawning occurs from May through September; females release their eggs into the water column. The larvae drift for about a month before settling into preferred habitat.

Spotted sand bass is a popular sport fish that has been reserved for sport fishermen only (no commercial fishery exists). Most fishing takes place from March through November, with peak catches occurring during the spawning season.

Spotted Sand Bass

SCIENTIFIC NAME
Paralabrax maculofasciatus
OTHER COMMON NAMES
bay bass, spotty, spotted bay bass
RANGE & HABITAT
*Monterey southward off rocky reefs
and artificial structure*
LENGTH & WEIGHT
To 23 in. and ~6 lb.
LIFE SPAN
To 14 years
DIET & SUGGESTED BAIT/LURES
*Feeds mainly on crabs, clams,
and small fishes. Try using live
anchovies for bait, or leadhead jigs,
swim baits, or wet flies*

to ~17 in.

Sargo may be found

from Santa Cruz southward off California, in bays and close to shore. They occupy depths from the surface to 130 ft., but are mostly caught in water about 25 ft. deep. The sargo's preferred habitat includes rocky areas, sometimes near sand, and around pilings or similar submerged structure.

Distinguishing Characteristics

Metallic silver, with a grayish tinge on the back and silvery below. Dark vertical bar running across the body. May occasionally be entirely bright yellow, orange, or pure white. Body oval shaped, with back elevated. Head with steep, nearly straight upper profile; small mouth, lips not thick. Dorsal fin without peak.

Life History & Other Notes

Sargo are bottom feeders, and eat a variety of small shrimps, crabs, clams and sea snails.

Spawning occurs in late spring and early summer. The young may be seen in late summer and fall in shallow water, schooling loosely with young salema and black croaker. They join adult sargo schools when they reach one year in age and about 5 inches in length.

Anglers fishing from rocky shores in Southern California often catch sargo. When pulled from the water this fish may make a pig-like grunting sound, hence the nicknames *croaker* and *grunt*. Sargo will take clam, mussel, shrimp, pieces of fish, or just about any type of animal bait. Because they tend to swim a few feet off the bottom in shallow water, they are a prime target for spear fishermen.

Sargo

SCIENTIFIC NAME
Anisotremus davidsonii

OTHER COMMON NAMES
China croaker, grunt

RANGE & HABITAT
Santa Cruz southward, usually south of Pt. Conception near rocky areas or pilings

LENGTH & WEIGHT
To ~17 in. and ~4 lb.

LIFE SPAN
To at least 15 years

DIET & SUGGESTED BAIT
Prefers shrimps, clams, crabs, and sea snails. Try clams, mussels, shrimp, or pieces of fish for bait.

White Seabass

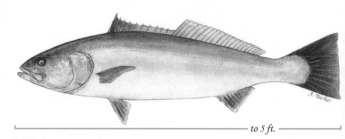

— to 5 ft. —

White seabass may

be found statewide off California, but are seldom seen north of San Francisco Bay. They usually travel in schools over rocky bottoms and through kelp beds.

Distinguishing Characteristics

Bluish to gray above with dark speckling, becoming silver below. Young will have several dark, vertical bars. Body elongate, head pointed. Mouth large, with a row of small teeth in the roof; lower jaw projects slightly. Ridge along the length of the belly.

Life History & Other Notes

The white seabass is the largest member of the croaker family off California, commonly exceeding 30 lb. White seabass feed on fishes, especially anchovies and sardines, and squid. Larger fish may also prey upon Pacific chub mackerel. A fish measuring 28 inches in length will average 5 years old and about 7½ lb., and will probably have participated in at least one spawning event.

White seabass are pursued primarily with live bait in relatively shallow water, but they will also take a fast-trolled spoon, artificial squid or bone jig. Live squid appear to be the best bait for white seabass, but large anchovies and medium-sized sardines are also good. At times, large white seabass will only bite on fairly large, live Pacific chub mackerel.

In 1983, CDFW and public partners began raising and releasing internally-tagged white seabass in hatcheries off Southern California to enhance the population. Returning white seabass heads to CDFW will assist in this effort.

White Seabass

SCIENTIFIC NAME
Atractoscion nobilis
OTHER COMMON NAMES
*weakfish, king croaker
sea trout (juveniles)*
RANGE & HABITAT
*Statewide, but mostly south of
San Francisco Bay.*
LENGTH & WEIGHT
To 5 ft. and ~90 lb.
LIFE SPAN
To at least 20 years
DIET & SUGGESTED BAIT/LURES
*Feeds on anchovies, sardines, squid,
Pacific chub mackerel. Try using the
above as bait, or a fast-trolled spoon,
jig, or swimbait*

— to 40 in. —

Ocean whitefish have

been caught from Fort Bragg southward off the California coast, but are rarely seen north of Point Conception. They prefer rocky bottom and kelp forest habitat in shallow areas, but may be found to a depth of 450 ft. Loosely aggregated schools of adults often are found at depths of 10 to 65 ft. Adults swim a few feet above the bottom, dropping down occasionally to search for food. Ocean whitefish are more abundant around offshore islands and banks than along the mainland coast.

Distinguishing Characteristics
Brownish-green to olive-green, very small scales. Very long dorsal fin that is almost the same height along its entire length; similarly long anal fin. Pectoral fins striped with yellow and blue.

Life History & Other Notes
Ocean whitefish eat an incredible variety of prey, including crabs, shrimp and other crustaceans, small octopi, squid, and fishes.

Spawning probably takes place during the fall, winter, and early spring. Young ocean whitefish have been caught in plankton nets miles offshore.

Many anglers feel that the ocean whitefish puts up the best battle for its size of any fish in the sea. Try fishing just above the bottom in rocky areas at depths between 60 and 100 ft. Likely fishing spots include offshore islands south of Santa Barbara County, Cortez Bank, and Tanner Bank. Spring, summer, and fall months offer excellent fishing for this species. Be aware of the sharp edges of the gill cover, which can inflict painful wounds.

Ocean Whitefish
SCIENTIFIC NAME
Caulolatilus princeps
OTHER COMMON NAMES
poor man's yellowtail
RANGE & HABITAT
*Statewide, but usually south
of Point Conception
over rocky reefs*
LENGTH
To 40 in.
LIFE SPAN
To 13+ years
DIET & SUGGESTED BAIT
*Feeds on crabs, shrimp, octopus,
squid, fishes. Try squid or fish
such as mackerel for bait*

141

Blacksmith

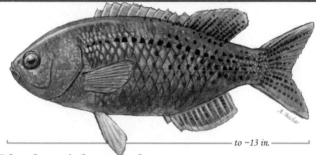

— to ~13 in. —

Blacksmith may be found from Monterey Bay southward off California, but are less common north of Point Conception. They prefer rugged, rocky bottom, and may also hover over steep banks and kelp beds, to a depth of 150 ft. At night, adult blacksmith seek shelter in small caves and crevices in the rock.

Distinguishing Characteristics
Blue-silver, with black spots on scales towards the posterior. Usually blue border on dorsal, anal, and tail fins.

Life History & Other Notes
Blacksmith feed on tiny shrimps and other crustaceans, and fish eggs. They are one of the most cold-water tolerant members of the damselfish family, whose members are mostly found in warmer waters to the south. Blacksmith are often found in large schools.

Most blacksmith are sexually mature by three years of age. Males construct nests under rock ledges or in small caves where the females lay sticky eggs. Male blacksmith aggressively guard the nest until the young hatch, in 3 to 6 days. After hatching, the young drift with the currents for about a month. Young blacksmith may be found in large schools in the open ocean.

Anglers should use little hooks that will fit into the blacksmith's small mouth. Try using tiny pieces of squid for bait.

Blacksmith
SCIENTIFIC NAME
Chromis punctipinnis
RANGE & HABITAT
Monterey Bay southward over rocky bottom, near steep banks, and in kelp beds
LENGTH & WEIGHT
To ~13 in.
DIET & SUGGESTED BAIT
Feeds on zooplankton, including tiny shrimps and fish eggs. Use small hooks baited with cut squid

Halfmoon

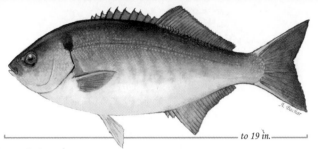

to 19 in.

Halfmoon are

primarily a Southern California fish, although they have been found as far north as the Klamath River in northern California. They are particularly common around the Channel Islands and Santa Catalina Island over shallow rocky areas and near kelp beds. Halfmoon have been observed as deep as 130 ft., but are most commonly taken in waters from 8 to 65 ft. deep.

Distinguishing Characteristics

Dark blue above, shading to blue-gray on the sides, becoming white below. Body oval, head blunt and rounded, mouth small. Tail half-moon shaped. No spines on gill cover. Soft rays of dorsal fin nearly hidden by a thick sheath of scales.

Life History & Other Notes

Halfmoon feed on a variety of plant and animal matter including algae, small invertebrates, and sponges. In the turbulent areas off rocky coasts they may be seen chasing and catching bits of surging seaweed.

Spawning takes place during the summer months. The eggs and young are free-floating, with the young generally found some distance from shore. Only adults are commonly found close to shore. Halfmoon reach maturity at about 7½ inches in length.

Halfmoon are easy to catch throughout the year. They are scrappy fighters, and good eating. Anglers fishing from rocky shores have good success for this species using mussels and shrimp; they are also caught on moss bait. Anglers fishing away from shore are most successful using fresh cut bait such as anchovy, sardine, or squid.

Halfmoon

SCIENTIFIC NAME
Medialuna californiensis

OTHER COMMON NAMES
Catalina blue perch, blue bass

RANGE & HABITAT
Klamath River south, but mostly in Southern California over shallow rocky areas and kelp beds

LENGTH & WEIGHT
To 19 in. and ~5 lb.

DIET & SUGGESTED BAIT
Feeds on algaes, small invertebrates and sponges. Try mussels, shrimp, anchovy, sardine, squid or moss for bait

---

143

Opaleye

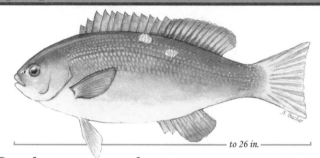

— to 26 in. —

Opaleye may be

found from San Francisco Bay southward off rocky shorelines and kelp beds. Young opaleye less than an inch long live in tidepools; they seek deeper water as they grow larger. The largest concentrations of opaleye may be found in about 65 ft. of water.

Distinguishing Characteristics

Dark olive green, usually with one or two white spots on each side of the back under the middle of the dorsal fin. Body oval, heavy and perch-like. Snout thick with an evenly rounded profile. Mouth small. Bright blue eyes.

Life History & Other Notes

Opaleye primarily eat marine algae with or without encrustations of organisms. Food items include feather boa kelp, giant kelp, sea lettuce, coralline algae, small tube-dwelling worms, and red crabs.

Spawning opaleye form dense schools in shallow water. The eggs and larvae are free-floating and may be found miles from shore. The young fish move close to shore and form schools of up to two dozen individuals, often in tidepools where they take advantage of a limited ability to extract oxygen from the air.

Few fish are harder to hook than the opaleye, and few fish will put up more fight, pound-for-pound. Long considered one of the better sport fishes, opaleye will take mussels, sand crabs, pieces of fish, and various invertebrates offered on a hook. Since opaleye are primarily vegetarians, some anglers find it easier to catch them using various mosses, or even green peas for bait.

Opaleye

SCIENTIFIC NAME
Girella nigricans

OTHER COMMON NAMES
buttoneye, green perch

RANGE & HABITAT
San Francisco Bay southwards, mostly south of Pt. Conception over shallow rocky areas and kelp beds

LENGTH & WEIGHT
To 26 in. and ~13 lb.

DIET & SUGGESTED BAIT
Feeds on algaes, marine worms, crabs. Try using sand crabs, mussels, pieces of fish, moss bait, or green peas on small hooks

---

California Sheephead

female

male — to 3 ft. —

California sheephead

are uncommon north of Point Conception, but have been caught as far north as Monterey Bay. They are generally taken in rocky kelp areas near shore, in waters from 20 to 100 ft. deep, although they may be found as deep as 280 ft.

Distinguishing Characteristics

This fish is a "protogynous hermaphrodite," which means that it begins life as a female, but then becomes a male in later life. **Female**: uniform pinkish red with white lower jaw. **Male**: Head and rear third of body black, mid-section red, lower jaw white. Males have a prominent, bulging forehead. Both sexes have unusually large, dog-like teeth.

Life History & Other Notes

Crabs, mussels, various-sized snails, squid, sea urchins, and sand dollars are typical food items for California sheephead.

Spawning takes place in early spring and summer. The young are brilliant red-orange, with two black spots on the dorsal fin and a black spot at the base of the tail fin. While young, the pelvic and anal fins are also black, trimmed in white. The young fade to a dull pink color when three to four inches long, and by the time they reach 6 to 8 inches long they have lost all spots and taken on typical female coloration.

California sheephead will take a variety of live and cut baits, such as anchovy or squid, fished on the bottom. Larger California sheephead may be taken using whole, live mackerel, also fished on the bottom. They are notable fighters.

California Sheephead

SCIENTIFIC NAME
Semicossyphus pulcher

OTHER COMMON NAMES
sheepie, goat, billygoat (large fish)

RANGE & HABITAT
Monterey Bay south, but usually south of Pt. Conception in rock/kelp bed areas

LENGTH & WEIGHT
To 3 ft. and ~36 lb.

LIFE SPAN
To 53 years

DIET & SUGGESTED BAIT
Feeds on crabs, mussels, snails, squid, sea urchin, sand dollar, sea cucumber. Try anchovy, squid or mackerel for bait

145

Albacore Tuna

to 5 ft.

Albacore tuna range

worldwide in temperate seas, and may be found coastwide off California at different times of the year. It is most frequently found in the upper layers of ocean waters, but will occasionally explore deeper, colder water in search of prey.

Distinguishing Characteristics

Dark gray to metallic blue to almost black on the back becoming white to gray below. Body tapers at both ends; head long, mouth fairly large. Pectoral fin extends well beyond anal fin. Albacore tuna can also be distinguished from bigeye or yellowfin tuna by comparing livers upon cleaning: albacore tuna liver is heavily striated (covered with blood vessels). It is the only tuna with both very long pectoral fins and a heavily striated liver.

Life History & Other Notes

Albacore prey varies depending upon where the fish are located and what is available. They seem to prefer small fishes, but will also take octopus, squid, and invertebrates such as shrimps and crabs.

Albacore tuna most likely spawn in the mid-Pacific during late summer. Off central and Southern California, they are usually found 20 to 100 miles offshore, when water temperatures reach 60° to 64° F. They are rarely taken near shore. Albacore tuna travel in loosely knit schools that can be located by trolling or observing surface signs (such as feeding birds). Once located, they are fished with hook and line using live anchovies for bait, or by trolling feathered jigs.

Albacore Tuna

SCIENTIFIC NAME
Thunnus alalunga

OTHER COMMON NAMES
longfin tuna, albie

RANGE & HABITAT
*Statewide, but usually off central and Southern California
20-100 miles offshore*

LENGTH & WEIGHT
To 5 ft. and 90 lb.

LIFE SPAN
To ~10 years

DIET & SUGGESTED BAIT/LURES
Feeds on fishes, squid, octopus, shrimp, crab. Try live anchovies or sauries for bait, or troll a feathered jig

Bigeye Tuna

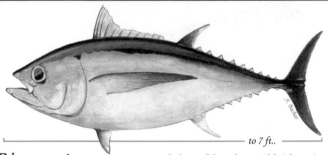

to 7 ft..

Bigeye tuna range

worldwide in warmer seas; they are only occasional visitors to Southern California. When they appear, bigeye tuna may be found on the California tuna grounds from June until November. They prefer water temperatures in excess of 70° F, but significant catches have occurred in water as cool as 65° F.

Distinguishing Characteristics

Dark metallic brownish-blue on the back becoming gray or whitish below. Often has a bluish stripe on the side. Body tapered at both ends (cigar-shaped). Head pointed, eyes relatively large. Pectoral fins extend past insertion of anal fin. Bigeye tuna can be distinguished from albacore or yellowfin tuna by comparing livers upon cleaning: bigeye tuna liver is lightly striated (covered with blood vessels) along the edges.

Life History & Other Notes

The diet of bigeye tuna includes fishes, squid, and crustaceans. Like most other tunas, they feed on whatever is most abundant wherever they happen to be.

Bigeye tuna do not spawn off California. A bigeye tuna weighing 159 lb. will produce over three million eggs per year. The young are fast growing and weigh about 45 lb. at maturity.

Bigeye tuna travel at great depths during the day, only rarely coming to the surface to feed, which makes them a challenging target for anglers. Try trolling marlin lures in an area where bigeye tuna are known to occur. Most bigeye tuna taken off California weigh under 200 lb.

Bigeye Tuna

SCIENTIFIC NAME
Thunnus obesus
OTHER COMMON NAMES
gorilla tuna, patudo, BET
RANGE & HABITAT
Statewide, but usually off central and Southern California
LENGTH & WEIGHT
To 7 ft. and 435 lb.
LIFE SPAN
To 9 years
DIET & SUGGESTED BAIT/LURES
Feeds on fishes, squid, and crustaceans. Try trolling marlin lures.

147

Dolphinfish

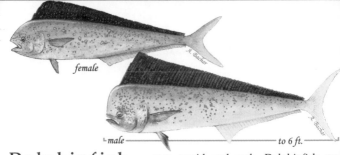

female

⌐ male ────────────── to 6 ft. ─┐

Dolphinfish, or

dorado as they are frequently called in California, range worldwide in temperate seas, and may be found coastwide off California during warm water years. Most catches occur in the Southern California Bight however, especially south of Los Angeles. Temperature seems to be an important factor in defining the range and possibly the movements of this fish. It is most frequently found in the warmer (over 68° F) upper layers of ocean waters, often near objects floating on the surface.

Distinguishing Characteristics

Blue to green above, sides yellowish with dark blue and green spots, but color is variable and changes rapidly. Bright yellow, deeply forked tail fin. Dorsal fin nearly continuous to the tail. White below. **Males**: Generally larger, heavier, with high bony crest presenting a blunt head profile. **Females**: Smaller, with curved head profile.

Life History & Other Notes

Dolphinfish mainly feed on fish, with flying fish being a favorite. They also eat jacks, mackerels, squid and crab. Dolphinfish are built for fast swimming, and can exceed speeds of 33 ft. per second.

Spawning is thought to occur year-round in waters above 75° F. Dolphinfish usually spawn south of the U.S., with larvae only collected off Southern California in warm water years. It is one of the fastest growing fish in the ocean.

The preferred fishing method for dolphinfish calls for using live bait, but they will also take trolled feather jigs, mackerel, or sardines.

Dolphinfish

SCIENTIFIC NAME
Coryphaena hippurus
OTHER COMMON NAMES
dorado, mahi mahi
RANGE & HABITAT
*Statewide, but usually
south of Los Angeles*
LENGTH & WEIGHT
To 6 ft. and 90 lb.
LIFE SPAN
To 5 years
DIET & SUGGESTED BAIT/LURES
*Feeds on fishes, squid, crab.
Try live bait fish such as
mackerel or sardines,
or troll feathered jigs*

Opah

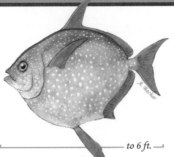

⊢—— *to 6 ft.* ——⊣

Opah are found

worldwide in warm and temperate seas, and may be found coastwide off California. Most landings occur in Southern California, especially during oceanic warm water events (such as El Niños). Opah inhabit ocean waters from the sea surface to a depth of 1,680 ft.

Distinguishing Characteristics

Iridescent silvery-blue with round to oval white spots. Snout, lips and fins brilliant red. Body oval and flattened. Small, toothless mouth that may protrude forward. Forked tail fin, yellow eye.

Life History & Other Notes

Opah are mid-water predators that eat squid, crustaceans, and fishes such as anchovy, lancetfish, and cutlassfish.

Very small opah, up to one-half in. long, resemble miniature adults in body form down to the number of fin rays. Young opah under 8 in. long are believed to be juveniles, although the exact size and age at sexual maturity is not known.

The opah's body type lends itself to a variety of traveling modes. It can swim slowly, accelerate quickly, and maintain cruising speeds easily, all which make it perfectly suited to its deep ocean existence.

Anglers targeting albacore tuna will occasionally land opah. Within California, opah are most often taken from the northern Channel Islands south to the border with Mexico. Opah are said to hit live bait such as anchovy or artificial lures with considerable fury. Their salmon-colored flesh is tasty, and can be prepared in a variety of ways. Smoked opah is excellent.

Opah

SCIENTIFIC NAME
Lampris guttatus

OTHER COMMON NAMES
African pompano, giant pompano

RANGE & HABITAT
Statewide, but usually off central and Southern California

LENGTH & WEIGHT
To 6 ft. and 160 lb.

DIET & SUGGESTED BAIT/LURES
Feeds on fishes, squid and crustaceans.
Try live anchovies for bait, or troll a feathered jig

149

Pacific Barracuda

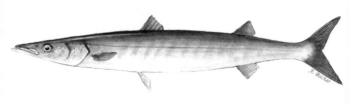

———————— to 5 ft. ————————

The Pacific barracuda

is usually found south of Point Conception but it may range much farther north, especially during oceanic warm water events. It prefers the upper water layers, from the surface to a depth of 60 ft.

Distinguishing Characteristics

Grayish black with a bluish tinge on the back, becoming silvery or white on the sides and belly. Tail yellowish. Body very elongate and slender, almost round. Mouth large with canine-looking teeth. Sharply pointed snout with projecting lower jaw. Dorsal fins widely spaced. Females with charcoal-black edge on pelvic and anal fins. Males with olive or yellow edge on pelvic and anal fins.

Life History & Other Notes

The Pacific barracuda preys mainly on anchovies and other small fishes.

The spawning season in Southern California may extend from April through September, but most spawning takes place in May, June and July. An individual female probably spawns more than once each season. Young barracuda up to six inches long are usually found in shallow water close to shore.

Most Pacific barracuda are taken with live bait fished at or near the surface; however, they will take an assortment of trolled artificial lures. If you see a large barracuda in the 10 lb. range, chances are it's a female. Three-pound Pacific barracuda are common, but generally fish of this size are large enough to put up a good fight. Use caution when landing a Pacific barracuda to avoid their needle-sharp teeth.

Pacific Barracuda

SCIENTIFIC NAME
Sphyraena argentea
OTHER COMMON NAMES
California barracuda, snake
RANGE & HABITAT
Statewide, but usually south of Point Conception
LENGTH & WEIGHT
To 5 ft. and 18+ lb.
LIFE SPAN
To 12 years
DIET & SUGGESTED BAIT/LURES
Feeds on anchovies and other small fishes. Try live bait such as anchovies or troll artificial lures

150

Pacific Bonito

to 40 in.

Pacific bonito may range throughout state waters, but they are most prevalent south of Point Conception. They sometimes arrive off California when the ocean warms in the spring, but may never show up if colder than normal water temperatures prevail.

Distinguishing Characteristics
Dark blue above, dusky on sides, silvery below. A number of slanted, dark stripes along the back (the only tuna-like fish in California to have this characteristic). Body cigar-shaped, head pointed and conical, mouth large with sharp teeth.

Life History & Other Notes
Pacific bonito prefer to feed on small fishes, such as anchovies and sardines. They sometimes include squid in their diet as well.

Pacific bonito may not spawn successfully off California every year; spawning generally takes place farther south. The bulk of Southern California spawning appears to take place from late January through May. The free-floating eggs take about three days to hatch.

Pacific bonito are excellent fighters and have hearty appetites. Once a school is aroused they will take almost any bait or lure that is tossed their way. Most Pacific bonito are taken by a combination of trolling and live bait fishing: schools are located by trolling feathers, and then live anchovies or pieces of squid are used for bait. Fishing for Pacific bonito generally takes place offshore in 300 to 600 ft. of water, but fishing next to kelp beds may also be productive when fish are found near shore.

Pacific Bonito
SCIENTIFIC NAME
Sarda chiliensis
OTHER COMMON NAMES
bonehead, bonita, Laguna tuna
RANGE & HABITAT
Statewide, but usually south of Point Conception
LENGTH & WEIGHT
To 40 in. and 25 lb.
DIET & SUGGESTED BAIT/LURES
Feeds on anchovies, sardines and other small fishes; try live anchovies or squid for bait; also try artificial lures

Skipjack Tuna

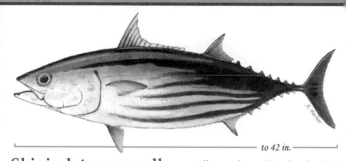

to 42 in.

Skipjack tuna usually

visit Southern California waters in the fall when ocean water temperatures are fairly warm (about 68° F) and the currents are either from the south or the southwest. They roam warm seas worldwide.

Distinguishing Characteristics

Dark blue to purple on the back, silvery or white below. Four to six dark horizontal stripes on the belly. Body cigar-shaped (tapers at both ends). Snout sharply pointed, mouth relatively large.

Life History & Other Notes

Skipjack tuna feed on fishes such as anchovies and sardines as well as squid; however, shrimp eggs and similar organisms are a major component of their diet.

Skipjack tuna do not spawn in waters off California; they prefer waters farther south. Spawning takes place during the summer months. A female skipjack tuna that measures 18½ in. long and weighs 5½ lb. can produce an estimated 113,000 eggs. Larger females can lay well over half a million eggs. The young fish grow rapidly, reaching 18 inches by their first birthday.

Skipjack tuna will bite a feathered jig eagerly, and will readily come to the boat when live anchovies are used as chum. Canned skipjack tuna is tasty, however fresh skipjack tuna is generally not considered desirable. This is a relatively small tuna, with most fish caught off California weighing between 2 and 12 lb., and the majority weighing 4 to 6 lb.

Skipjack Tuna

SCIENTIFIC NAME
Katsuwonus pelamis
OTHER COMMON NAMES
striped tuna, skippy
RANGE & HABITAT
Statewide, most commonly in Southern California
LENGTH & WEIGHT
To 42 in. and 26 lb.
LIFE SPAN
To 8+ years
DIET & SUGGESTED BAIT/LURES
Feeds on anchovies, sardines, squid, shrimp eggs. Try feathered jigs or live bait such as anchovies or sardines. Chum with live anchovies.

Striped Marlin

—— to 13+ ft.——

Striped marlin range

statewide off California, but are most common south of Point Conception. They may be found throughout the warm, tropical waters of the Indian and Pacific oceans. Striped marlin usually appear off the California coast in July, and remain through October.

Distinguishing Characteristics

Dark blue above, silver below, with 15 to 25 light blue bars or vertical rows of spots on sides.

Striped Marlin

SCIENTIFIC NAME
Tetrapturus audax

OTHER COMMON NAMES
striper, Pacific marlin

RANGE & HABITAT
Statewide, but usually south of Point Conception

LENGTH & WEIGHT
To 13+ ft. and 350 lb.

DIET & SUGGESTED BAIT/LURES
*Feeds on fishes, squid, crabs, shrimp.
Try trolling an artificial lure or use live bait*

Body elongate, upper jaw much extended, forming a rounded spear. Dorsal fin height equal to or greater than body depth. Body scaled, pelvic fins present. Two keels on root of the tail.

Life History & Other Notes

Striped marlin mostly feed on fishes, with squid, crabs and shrimp making up a smaller portion of their diet.

This fish uses its spear as both a defensive weapon and as an aid in capturing food. The striped marlin sometimes stuns its prey by slashing sideways with its spear rather than impaling the prey. Wooden boats have been rammed by billfish such as the striped marlin.

Off California, marlin are reserved as a sport-only fish (no commercial fishery exists). Most striped marlin are taken by trolling artificial lures in areas this fish is known to inhabit. Marlin swimming along the surface will strike at a lure trolled past the fish. Live bait also works well, but requires more effort since the fish must usually be spotted visually first in order to present the bait. Strikes generally result from properly presented live bait.

153

Swordfish

to 15 ft.

Off Southern California, swordfish are most commonly encountered between the mainland and the Channel Islands, although they occur worldwide in temperate and tropical seas.

Distinguishing Characteristics

Dark gray to black above, becoming gray to yellowish below. Body elongate. Upper jaw very much extended, forming a long, flat sword. Pelvic fins absent. One keel (small projection) at base of tail.

Life History & Other Notes

Swordfish feed on fishes, including anchovies, Pacific whiting, jack mackerel, rockfish, and pencil smelt. They will also eat squid.

Swordfish do not generally spawn off the coast of California, however in 1958 a female was harpooned off Santa Catalina Island that contained an estimated 50 million mature eggs.

Swordfish are taken from May through November, and occasionally landed in December. Most recreational fishing for swordfish involves visually searching for a fish that is "finning" (presenting itself at the surface) and then maneuvering a baited hook in front of it. Live Pacific mackerel or dead squid are the preferred baits.

Once hooked, swordfish are strong and stubborn fighters. Average encounters last more than four hours, although some fish are landed in a short time (10 to 15 min.) if the fish swims within gaffing distance of the boat early on. Most fish taken off Southern California weigh between 100 lb. and 300 lb., with an occasional fish weighing over 400 lb.

Swordfish

SCIENTIFIC NAME
Xiphias gladius

OTHER COMMON NAMES
broadbill, broadbill swordfish

RANGE & HABITAT
Statewide, most common from Point Conception south

LENGTH & WEIGHT
To 15 ft. and 1,182 lb.

LIFE SPAN
To 9+ years

DIET & SUGGESTED BAIT
Feeds on anchovies, Pacific whiting, jack mackerel, rockfishes, lanterfish, pencil smelt, squid. Try squid, live mackerel for bait

Bluefin Tuna

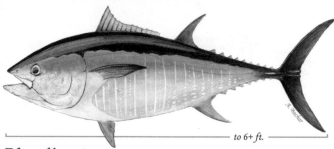

— to 6+ ft. —

Bluefin tuna may be found statewide off California, with the majority of fish landed weighing between 15 and 30 lb. (1- to 2-year-old fish). This tuna ranges worldwide in all but the very coldest seas.

Distinguishing Characteristics

Dark blue above, gray below. Body cigar-shaped and robust, head conical, mouth large. Relatively short pectoral fins. Bluefin tuna can be distinguished from other short-finned tunas by comparing the livers upon cleaning: bluefin tuna liver is heavily striated (covered with blood vessels). It is the only tuna with both relatively short pectoral fins and a heavily striated liver.

Life History & Other Notes

Bluefin tuna are seasonal visitors to California waters. While in the neighborhood, they feast mainly upon anchovies; they will also take other fishes such as Pacific whiting and sauries, as well as pelagic red crabs.

Bluefin tuna usually appear off California beginning in May. Since they are a temperate tuna, their availability to anglers depends on water temperatures hitting the 62° to 68° F range. They can be located by either trolling feathers or anchoring at a spot known to be frequented by bluefin tuna, and chumming with live anchovies. Once the fish are attracted, anglers use light line (12 lb. test or lighter), small hooks (no. 4 or smaller) and the "hottest" bait available that season, usually live anchovies or pieces of squid.

Bluefin Tuna

SCIENTIFIC NAME
Thunnus thynnus

OTHER COMMON NAMES
leaping tuna, football, BFT

RANGE & HABITAT
Statewide

LENGTH & WEIGHT
To 6+ ft. and 1000 lb.

LIFE SPAN
To 16 years

DIET & SUGGESTED BAIT/LURES
Feeds on fishes such as anchovy, Pacific whiting, and sauries; also invertebrates such as crabs. Try trolling an artificial lure or using live anchovies or pieces of squid

Yellowfin Tuna

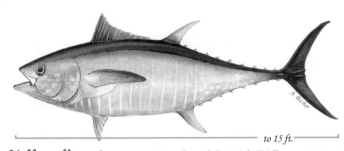

to 15 ft.

Yellowfin tuna are known to range as far north as Point Buchon in central California, but the best chance of finding them lies in Southern California waters when sea temperatures exceed 70° F.

Distinguishing Characteristics

Dark brownish-blue to blue to nearly black above, becoming gray or whitish below. Body tapers at both ends, head conical. Pectoral fins long, but do not extend beyond anal fin. Second dorsal fin and anal fin become elongated and sickle-shaped in larger fish. White vertical stripes and spots on belly. May be positively identified when cleaning the fish by checking the liver: Yellowfin tuna livers are smooth with no striations (blood vessels) on the surface.

Life History & Other Notes

The diet of the yellowfin tuna includes juvenile fishes, crustaceans, and squid. They are opportunistic feeders, taking whatever is most readily available in the area.

Yellowfin tuna spawn south of California, with some spawning taking place every month of the year. Young fish grow very rapidly. By the time they are 1½ years old

these fish weigh 7½ lb. on average; by 4 years old they can weigh around 150 lb.

Yellowfin tuna are fished in much the same manner as albacore tuna: feathered jigs are used to locate schools, and live anchovies are chummed to keep the fish around the boat. Most yellowfin tuna taken off California weigh 30 to 50 lb. (1- to 2-year-old fish), but occasionally fish over 200 lb. (over 10 years old) are landed.

Yellowfin Tuna

SCIENTIFIC NAME
Thunnus albacares

OTHER COMMON NAMES
Allison tuna, ahi, Pacific yellowfin

RANGE & HABITAT
To Point Buchon; generally in Southern California

LENGTH & WEIGHT
To 15 ft. and 450 lb.

LIFE SPAN
To ~10 years

DIET & SUGGESTED BAIT/LURES
Feeds on young fish, crustaceans, squid. Try live anchovies for bait, or a trolled, feathered jig

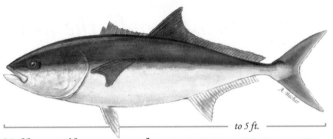

to 5 ft.

Yellowtail may be

found statewide off California, but most fish are taken south of Point Conception from the sea surface to a depth of 228 ft. Prime yellowtail areas include the La Jolla kelp beds, the area between Oceanside and Dana Point, Horseshoe Kelp, Palos Verdes Peninsula, Santa Catalina Island and San Clemente Island.

Distinguishing Characteristics

Olive-brown to brown above, dark horizontal stripe along side of body. Sides and belly are silvery. Fins yellowish; deeply forked yellow tail.

Life History & Other Notes

Yellowtail feed primarily during the day. They will eat anything that is abundant in the area, including pelagic red crabs, anchovies, squid and most small fishes.

Spawning occurs from June through October. Many yellowtail are sexually mature at two years; all will spawn by three years of age. A three-year-old female usually weighs about 10 lb. and can produce nearly half a million eggs; a 25 lb. female can produce more than a million eggs.

Most yellowtail are landed on boats that anchor in areas where yellowtail are known to aggregate. The fish are chummed to the boat with live anchovies. As the fish mill about the boat, anglers catch them using anchovies, mackerel or squid as bait. Anglers on small boats may take yellowtail by trolling jigs or feathers in areas where these fish occur.

Yellowtail

SCIENTIFIC NAME
Seriola lalandi

OTHER COMMON NAMES
California yellowtail, mossback, YT

RANGE & HABITAT
Statewide, but usually south of Point Conception

LENGTH & WEIGHT
To 5 ft. and 80 lb.

LIFE SPAN
To 12 years

DIET & SUGGESTED BAIT/LURES
Feeds on red crabs, anchovies, squid, small fishes.
Try using anchovies, squid, or mackerel for bait,
or trolling jigs or feathers.

157

Ocean Shellfish

*F*or most people, the word *fishing* brings to mind the image of an angler enticing a fish to bite a baited hook or artificial lure. However, ocean sport fishing opportunities in California are not limited to pursuing fishes with fins–shellfish (mollusks and crustaceans) are found everywhere along the 1,100-mile California coastline and offshore islands. In order to fully experience everything California has to offer to the sport angler, you'll need to put down your rod and reel and grab your clam fork or shovel, abalone iron, crab trap, hoop net, or dive bag.

No other state in the nation can compare to the Golden State in terms of variety of edible shellfish. From one end of the state to the other, shellfishing opportunities abound: shoveling frantically in pursuit of the fast-digging razor clam on a wave-swept Crescent City beach; breath-hold diving for a potential world-record red abalone in the cold waters off the Mendocino Coast; dropping a trap for Dungeness crab on opening day off Pacifica Pier; nighttime scuba diving for spiny lobster around Santa Catalina Island; or digging for world-famous Pismo clams at low tide on a Southern California beach. Or you can try your hand at diving for rock scallops and sea urchins; digging in soft bay mud for gaper clams – one of the largest clams on the West Coast–or prying mussels from the rocky intertidal zone.

Each of these fisheries is unique, and challenges the angler to improve on his or her skills. You'll need to familiarize yourself with new marine habitats, learn the role that the tides play in these animals' lives, and determine what works best for the quarry you're after. But as experience and knowledge of these fisheries increases, so too do the rewards reaped by the successful shellfisher – fresh Dungeness crab with sourdough bread, steamed lobster tails with drawn butter, and delicious New England style clam chowder are but a few of the culinary delights that await, not to mention the exhiliration of watching a California sunset from the beach, or simply spending time in the refreshing salt-sea air. For many Californians, partaking of the state's abundance of shellfish is as big a part of the outdoor experience as fishing with rod and reel.

courtesy E.W. Roberts III

California Spiny Lobster

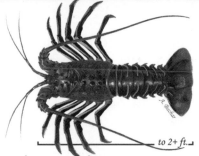

to 2+ ft.

California spiny lobster may be found from San Luis Obispo County southward off California. They prefer kelp beds and rocky areas off the Southern California mainland and around the Channel Islands, to depths of over 100 ft. Spiny lobsters often hide in holes and crevices in rugged rock surfaces for protection.

Distinguishing Characteristics

Brick-red to brown. Shell (*carapace*) with numerous forward-pointing spines. Two heavy, spiny antennae longer than the body, with two shorter antennules between the longer antennae. Ten legs. Small eyes set on stalks beneath long, sharp head spines. Two large, golden "false eye" spots below the actual eyes. Segmented tail ending in rounded fins.

Life History & Other Notes

California spiny lobsters feed on a wide range of plants and animals, and readily dine on most decaying materials.

Spawning occurs from March through August. Females may carry up to 800,000 coral-red eggs beneath their tail. Upon hatching, the tiny young drift with the currents for seven or eight months, going through twelve developmental stages before settling to the bottom as juvenile lobsters.

Many people catch spiny lobster using hoop nets (usually made of steel rings and netting) set on the sea floor and baited with fish remains. Skin and scuba divers also capture spiny lobsters with their hands.

California Spiny Lobster

SCIENTIFIC NAME
Panulirus interruptus
OTHER COMMON NAMES
bug
RANGE & HABITAT
San Luis Obispo County southward in nearshore rocky reefs and kelp
LENGTH & WEIGHT
To 2+ ft. and 26+ lb.
LIFE SPAN
To 30 years
DIET & SUGGESTED BAIT
Feeds on wide range of plant and animal material. Try fish carcasses for bait

Gaper Clams

to 10 in.

Both the Pacific gaper

clam and the fat gaper clam may be found on California beaches statewide. They prefer fine sand or firm, sandy-mud bottoms, especially in bays, estuaries, and more sheltered outer coastal areas. Humboldt Bay, Bodega Bay, Tomales Bay, Drakes Estero, Elkhorn Slough, and Morro Bay are popular digging areas.

Distinguishing Characteristics

This is the largest clam in California. Relatively thin, whitish shells with thick brown varnish-like coating that is often eroded. May be stained black in mud habitat. Black siphon extremely long, with a pair of flaps at the end. Siphon cannot be withdrawn into shell.

Life History & Other Notes

Gaper clams feed on plankton and bits of food they filter from the water. In intertidal clam beds, feeding occurs during the high tide period.

In central California, reproduction occurs year-round. The young swim freely until they settle onto the sea floor and begin to move downward into the sediments. Gaper clams grow about one inch per year for the first four years, after which the growth rate begins to slow.

Clammers generally use shovels to dig for these clams, which may be found as deep as four feet in sand or mud. In muddy areas, three-foot lengths of PVC pipe about 12 to 15 inches in diameter are often used to prevent holes from caving in. Gaper clams are generally used in clam chowder or fried and served as a main dish.

Gaper Clams

SCIENTIFIC NAME
Tresus nuttallii
Tresus capax

OTHER COMMON NAMES
horseneck clam, horse clam

RANGE & HABITAT
*Statewide in sand or firm,
sandy-mud bottoms*

WIDTH AND WEIGHT
To 10 in. and 5 lb.

LIFE SPAN
To 17 years

DIET
*Feeds on suspended plankton
and detritus*

161

Pacific Littleneck Clam

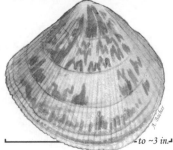

⊢ to ~3 in. ⊣

Six native species commonly known as littleneck clams or *chiones* are found on the California coast, but only one is found statewide: the Pacific littleneck clam. This clam is often found in coarse, sandy mud in bays, sloughs, and estuaries. On the open coast, they may be found near rocky points or reefs with small cobbles and coarse sand. They are usually easy to find at Malibu Point, Los Angeles County, in southern Orange County, and in Bodega and Tomales bays.

Distinguishing Characteristics

Yellowish-gray or gray in sloughs and bays, whitish along the open coast. Geometric patterns of wavy brown lines or blotches on sides; highly variable in color and pattern. Oval shells with well defined, radiating ribs and less prominent concentric ridges.

Life History & Other Notes

Pacific littleneck clams feed on plankton and bits of food suspended in the water. They are believed to spawn from late spring to early summer, and again in winter. The young drift with the currents for about three weeks, after which they settle and bury themselves in the sediments.

Because of their short siphons, this species is generally found within six inches of the surface. Harvesting is accomplished using rakes, shovels, garden hand forks, or trowels. Intertidal areas are usually targeted during daylight hours and at minus tides. Pacific littleneck clams are one of the most abundant clams on the West Coast, and are highly esteemed for food.

Pacific Littleneck Clam

SCIENTIFIC NAMES
Prototheca staminea

OTHER COMMON NAMES
rock cockle, bay cockle, rock clam

RANGE & HABITAT
Statewide in various habitats along the outer coast in mid-to-low intertidal zones and in bays, sloughs & estuaries

LENGTH
To ~3 in.

LIFE SPAN
To 10 years

DIET
Feeds on suspended plankton and detritus

Pismo Clam

to 7+ in.

Pismo clams have

historically been found as far north as Half Moon Bay; more recently, they have been difficult to find north of Pt. Conception. They prefer the intertidal zone, especially flat, sandy beaches on the open coast, but may be found offshore to a depth of 80 ft. Pismo clams may also be found in the entrance channels to bays, sloughs, and estuaries. Because they possess short siphons, they are generally found near the surface of the sand.

Pismo Clam

SCIENTIFIC NAME
Tivela stultorum
OTHER COMMON NAMES
giant tivela
RANGE & HABITAT
Half Moon Bay southward,
but mostly south of Pt.Conception
on flat, sandy beaches
LENGTH
To 7+ in.
LIFE SPAN
To 53 years
DIET
Feeds on suspended
plankton
and detritus

Distinguishing Characteristics

Pale beige to brown, but varies considerably in color and pattern. May have brown radiating marks on outer shell from hinge to rim. Shells thick, heavy, strong. Outside with fine, concentric growth lines, and a yellowish, tan, or green varnish-like coating. Inside of shell white.

Life History & Other Notes

Pismo clams feed on plankton and bits of food suspended in the water. Most Pismo clams spawn from June through September. Females may produce up to 20 million eggs per spawn. The young settle to the sandy bottom and attach themselves to sand grains by means of sticky threads. When the larvae have developed sufficiently, the threads disintegrate and the young clams bury themselves in the sand.

Clammers find these clams by probing wet, exposed sand with four- to six-tined gardening forks during low tide. The clams can also be found by looking for half-inch-long tufts of the hydroid *Clytia bakeri* that attaches to the shell and is exposed above the sandy beach surface.

163

Pacific Razor Clam

├─────────────── *to 7 in.* ───────────────┤

In California, the

Pacific razor clam may be found from the California-Oregon border southward to Pismo Beach, but they are most abundant in Del Norte and Humboldt counties. They prefer flat or gently sloping sandy beaches with moderate to heavy surf. The best Pacific razor clam beaches are in northern California, such as Clam Beach near Crescent City.

Distinguishing Characteristics

Shells red to reddish-brown, long, thin, fragile, and shiny. Heavy, yellowish, varnish-like coating. Foot without color.

Life History & Other Notes

Pacific razor clams feed on plankton and bits of food suspended in the water. They spawn in May and June, when water temperatures reach 55° F. The young settle to the sand about eight weeks after hatching, and grow rapidly for the first three years of life.

Pacific razor clams are excellent burrowers that depend on their digging speed for protection from wave shock. A clam laid on the surface of the beach will completely bury itself within seven seconds.

Clammers must dig quickly to capture these clams before they burrows to depths that are difficul to reach.

The Pacific razor clam is one o the tastiest food clams in California and is diligently pursued by sports men. When disturbed by heavy footsteps, these clams withdraw their siphons, leaving a character istic, slit-like opening in the sand Keeping a sharp eye out for thes openings will help clammers cap ture these quick-burrowing clams.

Pacific Razor Clam

SCIENTIFIC NAMES
Siliqua patula
OTHER COMMON NAMES
northern razor clam, razor clam
RANGE & HABITAT
Pismo Beach northward, but mostly north of Mendocino County on flat or gently sloping sand beaches exposed to surf
WIDTH
To 7 in.
LIFE SPAN
To 19 years
DIET
Feeds on suspended plankton and detritus

Nuttall Cockle

to 3+ in.

Nuttall cockles may

be found from San Diego northward in the mud or muddy sand of bays, sloughs, and estuaries, and in relatively shallow water in quiet, protected areas of the open coast. They are generally found on the surface of the beach or just beneath the surface. Nuttall cockles may be found at Pismo Beach, along the beach north of Morro Rock, and in Elkhorn Slough on Monterey Bay.

Distinguishing Characteristics

Smaller cockles are mottled with reddish-brown markings on buff colored shells; larger cockles (3+ in.) usually have a thick brown, varnish-like coating. Shells large and inflated, with about 34 bold, radiating, convex ribs separated by grooves. Exterior shell marked with concentric lines of growth, especially in larger cockles.

Life History & Other Notes

Nuttall cockles feed on plankton and other food particles suspended in the water. To reproduce, each individual Nuttall cockle produces both eggs and sperm.

When covered with water, the cockle opens its shell to feed, exposing its yellowish-white mantle edges which serve as a siphon for drawing in nutrient-laden water. At these times, Nuttall cockles are easier to spot and pick out of the mud. These cockles are highly esteemed for food.

It is always advisable to check with the California Department of Public Health for shellfish advisories ((800) 553-4133) before consuming any cockle, clam, or other bivalve.

Nuttall Cockle

SCIENTIFIC NAME
Clinocardium nuttalli

OTHER COMMON NAMES
basket cockle, heart cockle, quahog

RANGE & HABITAT
San Diego northward in muddy sand beaches of bays, sloughs and estuaries

WIDTH
To 3+ in.

LIFE SPAN
To 16 years

DIET
Feeds on suspended plankton and detritus

165

California Mussel

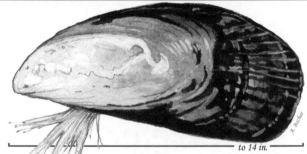

to 14 in.

California mussels are common along California's rocky beaches. They attach themselves to rocks, sometimes in great masses between tide lines where they are directly exposed to the surf. They may also attach to pier pilings on the outer coast along with the smaller bay mussel, and are infrequently found inside sheltered bays.

Distinguishing Characteristics

Shell covered with heavy, black, varnish-like coating (when worn off in older specimens, the blue shell beneath may be seen). Shells long, with hinge at smaller end. Exterior of shell with about 12 radiating ridges and numerous concentric growth lines. Interior of shell bluish-black, iridescent.

Life History & Other Notes

California mussels feed on plankton and other food particles suspended in the water. Spawning occurs year-round, with peaks in July and December. Fertilized eggs develop into free-swimming young that eventually change form and settle onto any available hard surface. New arrivals unable to find open rock faces may attach themselves to other mussels, which may prevent the mussels beneath from feeding and eventually result in their deaths.

During the summer months, the microscopic organism *Alexandrium catenella* eaten by mussels renders their viscera (guts) poisonous to humans. It is always advisable to check with the California Department of Public Health regarding the annual mussel quarantine ((800) 553-4133) before consuming mussels.

California Mussel

SCIENTIFIC NAMES
Mytilus californianus

OTHER COMMON NAMES
*big mussel, sea mussel
rock mussel*

RANGE & HABITAT
*Statewide on rocky habitat,
sometimes on pilings*

LENGTH
To 14 in.

DIET
*Feeds on suspended
plankton
and detritus*

166

Giant Rock Scallop

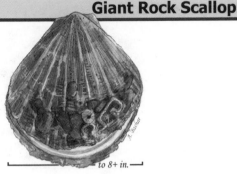

— to 8+ in. —

The giant rock scallop may be found statewide from the lower intertidal area to a depth of 100 ft. They typically inhabit offshore reefs, although concrete pier pilings and rock jetty entrances to bays in Southern California are also favored habitats.

Distinguishing Characteristics

Shell thick and heavy, lower shell often resembles the rock to which it is attached. Upper shell rough, with many radiating ribs and short, fluted spines. Often riddled with holes from boring sponges, worms, and bivalves. Irregular oval shape, orange- or green-tentacled mantle. Interior hinge area purple.

Life History & Other Notes

The giant rock scallop feeds on plankton and suspended bits of food. Young rock scallops drift with the currents until they are about five weeks old, at which time they settle, sometimes temporarily, on hard surfaces. Rock scallops are able to swim like ordinary scallops until they reach about six months of age and an inch in diameter, when they attach themselves permanently to suitable rocks or other stationary objects.

Giant rock scallops are usually pried from their attachment surfaces with long metal bars known as *abalone irons*. In Southern California they are taken by divers in rocky areas of the outer coast. In northern California they may be found close to shore in shallow water, where abalone shore-pickers can find them at low tide.

Giant Rock Scallop

SCIENTIFIC NAME
Crassadoma gigantea
OTHER COMMON NAMES
rock scallop
purple-hinged scallop
RANGE & HABITAT
Statewide on offshore reefs,
concrete pier pilings
or rock jetties
WIDTH
To 8+ in.
DIET
Feeds on suspended
plankton
and detritus

167

Dungeness Crab

to 9 in.

In California, the Dungeness crab ranges from the California-Oregon border southward to Santa Barbara, however they are uncommon south of Point Conception. This species prefers sandy or sand-mud bottom, but may be found in almost any sea floor habitat. They range from the intertidal zone to a depth of at least 750 ft., but are not abundant beyond 300 ft.

Distinguishing Characteristics

Dark rusty red. Broadly oval shell (*carapace*) with distinctive lighter markings, and modestly serrated front edge. Ten legs, front pincers largest, last segment of legs may be paler with white tips.

Life History & Other Notes

Dungeness crab feed on a variety of food sources, but prefer clams, fish, and other crustaceans (including other, smaler Dungeness crab) when available.

Female molting and mating occurs from February through June off California. Females may carry up to two million eggs under a flap on their belly. The eggs hatch between November and February,

with newly hatched young passing through six developmental stages before reaching adult form and settling into nearshore areas. Although inshore-offshore movement of Dungeness crab has been observed, most move less than 10 miles from where they settle.

Divers capture Dungeness crab by hand, but most crabbers capture them using traditional hoop nets or traps from jetties, piers, or boats. Clams and fish carcasses are favorite bait.

Dungeness Crab

SCIENTIFIC NAME
Metacarcinus magister

OTHER COMMON NAMES
Dungie, market crab

RANGE & HABITAT
Mostly north of Pt. Conception on sandy or sand-mud bottom

WIDTH
To 9 in.

LIFE SPAN
To 8 years

DIET & BAIT
Feeds on clams, fish, and other crustaceans, but will adapt to whatever is available. Try clams or fish carcasses for bait

---

Red Rock Crab

to 8 in.

The red rock crab

may be found statewide in shallow coastal areas and bays, on rocky or reef-type habitat. They range from the intertidal zone to depths of 300 ft. or more.

Distinguishing Characteristics

Orangish-red to darker, rusty red. Shell (*carapace*) with heavily serrated front edge. Ten legs; large red pincers with black tips, eight remaining legs lighter.

Red Rock Crab

SCIENTIFIC NAMES
Cancer productus

OTHER COMMON NAMES
rock crab

RANGE & HABITAT
Statewide in coastal areas and bays, on rocky or reef-type habitat

LENGTH
To 8 in.

LIFE SPAN
To 6 years

DIET & BAIT
Feeds a variety of invertebrates including snails, clams, abalone, barnacles, oysters. Try clams for bait

---

Life History & Other Notes

Red rock crabs are both predators and scavengers, feeding on a variety of other invertebrates. Their strong, crushing claws allow them to prey on heavy-shelled animals such as snails, clams, abalone, barnacles and oysters.

In Southern California, mating is most common in the spring but occurs throughout the year. Females carry egg masses containing up to four million eggs on their abdomen. The eggs hatch in early fall. The larvae undergo six developmental stages before settling to the bottom as juvenile crabs.

Gear for taking red rock crab ranges from a diver's or shore picker's hands to baited hoop nets and traditional traps (traditional traps, called "crab pots", may only be used legally north of Point Arguello). Hoop nets and traps may be fished from piers, jetties, and boats. Likely fishing areas include the shallow, nearshore open coast and in bays.

169

Red Abalone

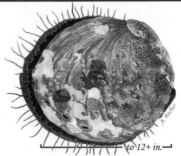

to 12+ in.

Red abalone may be found coastwide off California, however in Southern California (where their take is currently prohibited) they keep to cooler upwelling locations along the mainland coast and the northern Channel Islands. In central and northern California they may be found from the intertidal zone to depths nearing 75 ft. Red abalone prefer rugged, rocky habitat close to kelp beds, a primary food source.

Distinguishing Characteristics

Dull brick-red shell. Surface lumpy, usually covered with encrusting marine growth. Inside shell iridescent, highly polished. Outer lip of shell usually with narrow red rim. Shell holes slightly raised and oval, three to four usually open. Body and foot smooth, usually black. Edges of foot scalloped, thin black tentacles extend beyond edge of shell.

Life History & Other Notes

Abalone prefer to feed on drifting blades of kelp, especially giant and bull kelp.

Spawning season lasts from October through February in north-ern California, while in Southern California spawning occurs year-round. Male and female abalone release their sperm and eggs into the sea at the same time, and so must be located fairly close together for successful reproduction.

The red abalone fishery is strictly regulated (be sure to check regulations beforehand). Abalone are pried from rocks by shore pickers or skin divers using long metal bars known as *abalone irons*.

Red Abalone

SCIENTIFIC NAME
Haliotis rufescens
OTHER COMMON NAMES
red ab
RANGE AND HABITAT
Statewide, most common in northern California
LENGTH & WEIGHT
To 12+ in. and 10+ lb.
LIFE SPAN
To 30 years
DIET
Feeds mostly on bull kelp (northern California) and giant kelp (Southern California)

Red Sea Urchin

to 8+ in.

A cousin of the sea star, brittle star, and sand dollar, the red sea urchin may be found statewide off California wherever conditions are favorable. They generally prefer rugged, rocky habitat near kelp forests.

Distinguishing Characteristics

Deep red or red-brown, sometimes purple. Hard, rounded outer shell (called a *test*). Movable spines and small pincers. Tube feet between spines. Mouth at base, consisting of a five-plated jaw structure commonly called an *Aristotle's lantern* when found washed up on the beach.

Life History & Other Notes

Red sea urchins eat a variety of plants, but prefer leafy algae such as giant kelp and bull kelp.

The red sea urchin usually spawns in the winter in Southern California, and during the spring and summer in northern California. However, the time of spawning is often dependent on ocean temperature and other variables. Male and female urchins release their sperm and eggs into the sea at the same time, and so must be located fairly close together for reproduction to be successful. Female urchins may release up to several million eggs at one time. The young drift with the currents before settling to the bottom.

The gonads of both female and male red sea urchins are referred to as roe, or *uni* in Japan where it is considered a delicacy. Roe from Southern California sea urchins is considered superior by many because of its smaller size and sweeter taste.

Red Sea Urchin

SCIENTIFIC NAMES
Strongylocentrotus franciscanus

RANGE AND HABITAT
Statewide

WIDTH
To 8+ in. (including spines)

LIFE SPAN
To 120+ years

DIET
*Feeds on giant kelp
(Southern California)
or bull kelp (northern California)
but will adapt to
whatever is available*

171

Humboldt Squid

A. Bachar

— to 12 ft. —

Humboldt squid,

often referred to as *jumbo squid*, are occasional visitors to Southern California. Their arrival usually heralds a warm-water influx or event (such as an *El Niño* event) off the California coast. In most years, their range extends north only to Point Conception, however they have been caught statewide. Humboldt squid may be found from surface waters to a depth of 1,500 ft.

Distinguishing Characteristics

Deep purplish-red to reddish-brown; color variable. Mantle very large and thick-walled, with two broad, muscular fins. Eight shorter tentacles; two longer arms with extended tips and 100 to 200 very small, closely packed suckers.

Life History & Other Notes

Humboldt squid feed on the larvae of fishes such as lanternfish, sardines, mackerel and sauries. It also feeds on crustaceans, and on smaller squid.

Humboldt squid become sexually mature between two and six months of age (earlier for males than females). Their migration movements are not well understood, but it is believed that in the northern hemisphere they move southward to breed, and northward in search of prey. Young squid grow at different rates depending on environmental conditions at the time of hatching, but they are generally extremely fast-growing.

Recreational fishermen targeting jumbo squid often use large weighted squid jigs, typically adorned with glowing beads. Jigs may be fished to a depth of 1,000 ft.

Humboldt Squid

SCIENTIFIC NAME
Dosidicus gigas

OTHER COMMON NAMES
jumbo squid, squirt

RANGE AND HABITAT
To Point Conception, but occasionally farther north

LENGTH & WEIGHT
To 12 ft. (including arms) and 110 lb.

LIFE SPAN
To 1 year

DIET & SUGGESTED LURES
Feeds on young lanternfishes, sardines, mackerels, and sauries, as well as crustaceans and other squid. Try weighted squid jigs.

California Market Squid

A. Bachar

to 12 in.

The California market

squid may be found in ocean waters statewide. They are most often seen during spawning events when they congregate in semi-protected bays and near offshore islands, usually over sand bottom near rocky outcroppings. When not mating they move offshore into deep ocean waters, diving to 1,500 ft. during the day and returning to the surface to hunt at night. California market squid generally stay within 200 miles of shore.

Distinguishing Characteristics
Sand to cream color with changeable brownish to iridescent markings. Long, tapering, cigar-shaped body. Mantle with two large, elongate, triangular fins.

Life History & Other Notes
California market squid feed on small crustaceans, snails, worms, small fishes, and squid.

Mass spawning takes place from around April through November in central California waters, and from October through April in Southern California waters. Spawning may occur year-round, however. Females attach white, cigar-shaped egg capsules to the sea floor that may each contain up to 300 eggs. These mass spawnings often cover large areas of the sea floor.

California market squid is used to make the seafood dish *calamari*, and is considered a delicacy. It is also a very effective and popular bait for fish such as white seabass and yellowtail. Try jigging for market squid at night from a local pier or from a boat during high tide, using a small light as a "squid magnet."

California Market Squid

SCIENTIFIC NAMES
Loligo (doryteuthis) opalescens

OTHER COMMON NAMES
market squid

RANGE AND HABITAT
Statewide

LENGTH
To 12 in. (including arms)

LIFE SPAN
To 9 months

DIET & SUGGESTED LURES
Feeds on small crustaceans, snails, worms, small fishes, smaller squids. Try jigging for them at night during a high tide using a light source as an attractant.

173

Glossary

Anadromous
Describes fish that begin life in fresh water, migrate to salt or brackish water for a portion of their life, and eventually return to fresh water to spawn.

Bivalve
Mollusk that has two shells hinged together, such as a clam or scallop.

Carapace
The shield covering the upper surface of the body of various crustacean species (for example, the broad shield forming the upper body cover of crabs, and of the front portion of lobsters and crayfish).

Crustacean
Predominantly aquatic arthropods of the class Crustacea, including lobsters, crabs, shrimps, and barnacles, characteristically having a segmented body, a chitonous exoskeleton, and paired, jointed limbs.

Drainage
The area within which all surface water will normally gather in a single conduit or water course.

Foot (clam, abalone)
The fleshy, muscular part of a mollusk that aids in movement and, in the case of abalone, securing the animal to it's substrate for protection.

Fry
The young of fishes.

Habitat
An area with a combination of resources (including food, cover, water, and environmental conditions) that promotes occupancy by individuals of a given species and allows those individuals to survive and reproduce.

Hybrid
The offspring of genetically dissimilar parents or stock, such as the offspring produced by breeding different varieties or species of fish.